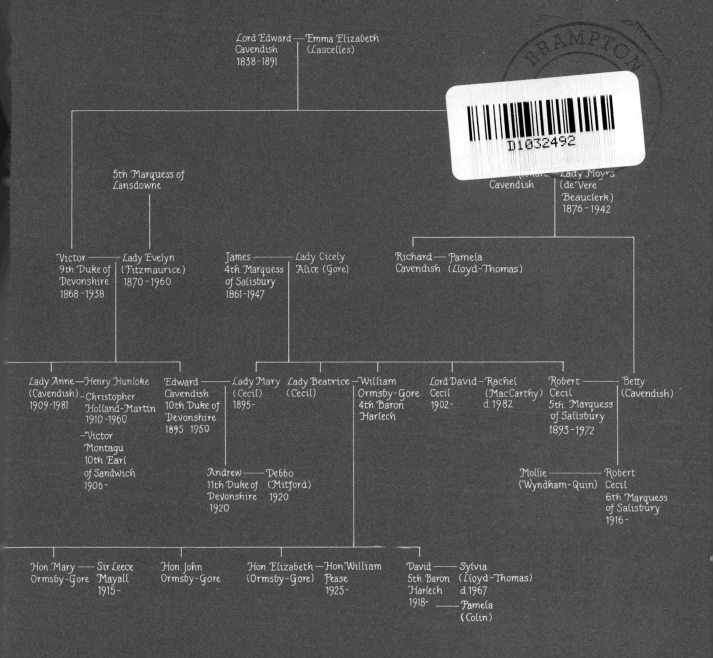

Lord Edward — Emma Elizabeth
Cavendish    (Lascelles)
1838-1891

5th Marquess of
Lansdowne

............. — Lady Moyra
Cavendish    (de Vere
             Beauclerk)
             1876-1942

Victor ——— Lady Evelyn
9th Duke of  (Fitzmaurice)
Devonshire   1870-1960
1868-1938

James ——— Lady Cicely
4th Marquess Alice (Gore)
of Salisbury
1861-1947

Richard — Pamela
Cavendish (Lloyd-Thomas)

Lady Anne —Henry Hunloke    Edward ——— Lady Mary   Lady Beatrice  —William      Lord David —Rachel      Robert ——— Betty
(Cavendish)                 Cavendish  (Cecil)      (Cecil)         Ormsby-Gore   Cecil      (MacCarthy)  Cecil       (Cavendish)
1909-1981  —Christopher     10th Duke of 1895-                      4th Baron     1902-      d.1982       5th Marquess
           Holland-Martin   Devonshire                             Harlech                              of Salisbury
           1910-1960        1895  1950                                                                  1893-1972
           —Victor
           Montagu          Andrew ——— Debbo                                                  Mollie ——————— Robert
           10th Earl        11th Duke of (Mitford)                                            (Wyndham-Quin)  Cecil
           of Sandwich      Devonshire  1920                                                                 6th Marquess
           1906-            1920                                                                             of Salisbury
                                                                                                            1916-

Hon. Mary —— Sir Leece    Hon John          Hon Elizabeth —Hon William   David ——— Sylvia
Ormsby-Gore  Mayall       Ormsby-Gore       (Ormsby-Gore)  Pease         5th Baron (Lloyd-Thomas)
1915-                                                       1925-         Harlech   d.1967
                                                                          1918-  —Pamela
                                                                                  (Colin)

# Harold Macmillan
## *A Life in Pictures*

# Harold Macmillan
## *A Life in Pictures*

*Text by Ruth Dudley Edwards*
*Introduction by Alistair Horne*

MACMILLAN LONDON

Design by Robert Updegraff
Picture Research by Caroline Alcock

ISBN 0 333 349873

First published 1983 by
Macmillan London Limited
London and Basingstoke

Associated companies in Auckland, Dallas,
Delhi, Dublin, Hong Kong, Johannesburg,
Lagos, Manzini, Melbourne, Nairobi,
New York, Singapore, Tokyo, Washington
and Zaria

Filmset in Plantin by
Filmtype Services Limited
Scarborough, North Yorkshire

Printed in Hong Kong

Page i: *Arthur, self (centre) and Daniel on holiday
at West Cliff Dean, on the Isle of Wight.*

Page ii: *This sketch by James Gunn was for a
portrait in 1962 for Oxford University, which hangs
in Balliol. A copy hangs in the Carlton Club in the
private dining-room known, embarrassingly, as the
Macmillan Room.*

# Contents

# Introduction

## by Alistair Horne

*'I have been fortunate enough to sit at your feet, as it were, and to listen, spellbound, to the way in which you describe events and people in terms of their historical perspective . . .'*

The Prince of Wales praising Harold Macmillan during a speech accepting a civil law degree from Oxford University

Poetry, so Wordsworth once remarked, derives its origin from 'emotion recollected in tranquillity'. Perhaps one of the few and most prized consolations of old age is the joy of being able to recollect in tranquillity the people and events of the past.

It was in his old age (*aetat* eighty-five) that – apart from the sporadic encounters of author and publisher – I first got to know Harold Macmillan. To my considerable surprise, out of the blue I had been invited to be his official biographer. Flattering a proposition as it was, I was distinctly uneasy about my qualifications to take on such a task. Finally it was agreed that I should go down to Birch Grove, so that subject and biographer could 'look at each other'. As we walked round and round the garden, lovingly laid out by his redoubtable American mother, Nellie Macmillan, and improved by Lady Dorothy, I began to realise that he was just about as diffident as I was. I recall making some flip remark about my knowing all too little about British party politics, and not even being sure that I was a good Tory. He replied, 'Nor was I!' The ice was broken; we went into the house, and there began several of the most rewarding (though demanding) years of my life.

Our relationship was a curious one. Few biographers of eminent public figures have the enviable good fortune to have access to the memory of their victim during his lifetime, and Macmillan enjoyed introducing me to friends as being 'a cross between Boswell and

Torquemada!' We would work often three days at a stretch, very professionally, recording exhaustively on tape his answers to my inquisitions. As it unfolded, I did to some extent come to see his long life in terms of a photograph album.

Spanning from the horse-drawn trams of Queen Victoria's day to the Space Shuttle and silicon chips, the recollections which I drew out of him imparted a special flavour to the personalities he had known. Birch Grove seemed full of the ghosts of the great and the good, the high and the mighty, and of the memorabilia of their visits during the Macmillan era. There were the foreign potentates like Eisenhower, Adenauer, de Gaulle, Khrushchev, Diefenbaker, Verwoerd, Nehru, Nkrumah and Kennedy. Some, like Nkrumah and Khrushchev, had been deposed; some, like Verwoerd and Kennedy, assassinated. (In the library there still stands the rocking chair, draped in its original rug, which had been acquired for the President's bad back during his last stay just five months before the assassination.) There were Prime Ministers whom Macmillan had served with, or been followed by (six had ruled since he entered the house in 1924, while already another five have succeeded him since he relinquished office in 1963).

Of the *Pastmasters* (as he dubbed them in a book of his own) undoubtedly it was Lloyd George and Churchill who had most influenced him, and Churchill who – among all those in his life – he most venerated. There were the military paladins – Alexander, Monty, Smuts and Mountbatten; and there were his own contemporaries and juniors – Eden, 'Rab' Butler, Selwyn Lloyd, Alan Lennox-Boyd, Antony Head – many of whom (and younger than Macmillan) had died off at an accelerating tempo over the past years while he strode on – though frail in body – with an amazing youthfulness of spirit and mind. And there were the members of the family, a predeceased daughter and grandson, and – above all – the wife to whom he was devoted, Dorothy, who died within little more than two years of his resignation, just when they might have looked forward together to the fruit of all the arduous times transmuted into long years of peaceful and contented retirement.

In the course of our conversations, Harold Macmillan managed to make all those ghosts spring to life before my eyes, with a vividness that often seemed lacking in his own six-volume memoirs. He would speak of his contemporaries, greater and lesser, sometimes in pungent and mischievous terms, but always perceptively and more often than not concluding on a note of affection and charity. I never heard him express rancour (except, possibly, when discussing the lords of the media); not even towards de Gaulle, the man whom he had saved time and again during the war from the combined wrath of Churchill and Roosevelt, yet who – twenty years later – had so bitterly injured him through vetoing Britain's entry into the EEC.

So the procession of historical figures filed past my eyes, as in the pages of this picture book. During our long sessions with the tape recorder, I found Macmillan's memory in general so sharply focused – despite his four score and more years – as not to need photos, or even notes, to help prompt it. To return to Wordsworth's proposition, for the purpose of recollection in tranquillity of the past, there is no happier adjunct than scrap-books or photograph albums, but Harold Macmillan's chief purpose in assembling these pictures was for the benefit of the outside world, rather than his own. And the collection is instructive. Apart from reminding us of the people and events that, woven together, composed Macmillan's world embracing nine-tenths of a century, they also tell us more about the author than many words can. We see the many facets of one of the most complex characters in British public life – the crofter's grandson and the duke's son-in-law, the soldier and the scholar, the publisher and the politician, the *bon viveur* and the devout high churchman. We also see his progress from the gawky, insecure young MP of the Twenties and Thirties to 'Supermac', 'Macwonder' and to Britain's most urbane and 'unflappable' statesman.

The camera is revealing. Macmillan was what is known as a 'late developer'; he was approaching fifty when he first came into his own as Churchill's envoy to North Africa in 1942 and sixty-three when he became Prime Minister; while after he left No. 10, the evolutionary process by no means halted. The 'Supermac' image was, in fact, but a glaze on the portrait, achieved only after a lifelong struggle against innate diffidence, insecurity and sometimes acute depression. It took me a long time to believe that, even as PM, he would sometimes be physically sick with nerves on the day preceding a major speech. But it was quite true. All this is suggested in the inelegant, almost shabby dress of the earlier photographs, the baggy trousers that would have dismayed any high street tailor in Stockton, the rimless glasses, the unkempt bushy moustache, the teeth in grave disarray. What a contrast, in a photograph taken in Algiers in 1943, between the dapper, glamorous Anthony Eden and an almost unrecognisable Macmillan, his jacket unfashionably buttoned up to the top! (p. 52). Which of the two could one have predicted to become the most successful Prime Minister of his generation, which the tragic failure? Here is another clue to be observed; whether in a group at pre-1914 Balliol (pp. 14–15), or in a fishing party with a young Lady Dorothy (p. 26) in 1920 Canada, or with the potentates at Casablanca and Cairo in 1943 (pp. 62 and 63), Macmillan always somehow seems to be standing shyly in the back row or at the corner of the picture, looking in. At the 'Allied Grand Strategy Conference' in Casablanca, revealingly, Churchill's Minister Resident is once again out on the fringe, while a thrustful young Vice-Admiral Mountbatten, who suffered from no such pangs of diffidence, is to be found immediately behind the master (p. 62).

Then, after he becomes Prime Minister, somewhere between the triumphant Commonwealth tour of 1958 and the equally triumphant General Election of 1959, a new, self-confident Macmillan appears on the scene. The schoolmasterly glasses have disappeared, the disorderly moustache has been rigorously pruned, the smile is no longer toothy and half-apologetic, and he is wearing a spruce new suit. The first incumbent of No. 10 to emerge as a 'TV personality' has arrived, and the success is almost immediate.

Always reticent about anything that concerns his private self, Macmillan admitted to having been wounded three times in the Great War, in which he conducted himself with great courage. He did, however, by my reckoning, receive five separate wounds, and they continued to be a great deal more painful than he would ever admit. In a photograph of electioneering at Stockton in 1930 (p. 45) the candidate (looking only marginally less down-at-heel than his depressed constituents) is shown with his right hand hanging curiously limp. This was in fact the hand shot through by a German bullet at the Battle of Loos, and in his later life it was to provide the source of much unkind talk about the Prime Minister having a 'handshake like a wet fish'. Characteristically, Macmillan never revealed the cause, even to his closest colleagues.

In this book, there are many other photographs that one might single out as being evocative, revealing, or telling a particular story better than words could. There is, for instance, the South African banquet scene during the historic 'Wind of Change' visit of 1960; the empty chair between Macmillan and Verwoerd is eloquently symbolic (p. 140). There is the photograph of Macmillan with Secretary of State Dulles in a dressing gown, mortally ill with cancer in the Walter Reed Hospital (p. 103). It was a scene that signalled the end of an era when – in the wake of Suez – the Anglo-American 'Special Relationship' had reached its lowest ebb since World War II; while a sunny pose with J.F.K. on the steps of the White House (p. 133) relates implicitly the miraculous way in which Macmillan had restored the 'Special Relationship' to a level that has never been achieved since – or, for that matter, had even existed previously, during the Roosevelt–Churchill honeymoon period. There is a suggestion of the electoral magician in the photo of the 1959 election; no TV yet, but with the campaigner putting his voice over on a 45 r.p.m. disc

(p. 126). And there are the revealing family shots: the stern and fiercely ambitious Midwestern grandmother outside Birch Grove; a politically dedicated Lady Dorothy campaigning for her husband in the Twenties, Thirties and Fifties – perhaps one of his greatest assets; and then the solitary widower wandering amid spring flowers at Birch Grove.

Well after his retirement, in his old age when I met him, Harold Macmillan seemed to take on a remarkable new lease of life, just at a time when other men would give up. Although lonely in his lifestyle, he developed a boundless range of interests in the outside world. Perhaps this contained the secret of his mental and spiritual youthfulness. As a conversationalist – in which he has no peer – he is always astonishingly 'with it', offering views on current events that are refreshingly off-beat, loaded with humanity and humour, the latter often tinged with Celtic blackness. After a few minutes of his company, one begins to feel one is talking to a contemporary, and a particularly bright and amusing one at that. He took to travelling widely: to Nigeria in 1975, to China in 1979 (where, when offered a wheelchair, he stumped his thoughtful hosts by replying, 'I'd much rather have a brandy and soda!'), to the USA in 1980 (describing himself as a salesman for Macmillan's new edition of *Grove's Dictionary of Music and Musicians*) and to Oman and Jordan in 1983 following his eighty-ninth birthday. He came out of his corner to speak frequently (and with even greater mastery than before 1963), and – whether to the Washington Smithsonian in 1980 or at the Carlton Club in 1982 (p. 178), he regularly brings the house down in laughter, and in tears. He keeps closely in touch with Mrs Thatcher, and with the Tory back benches, and greatly enjoys affairs of state, such as meetings of the Privy Council (between pp. 174 and 175) or of the Order of Merit (the one honour he ever truly coveted) (p. 167)

But his greatest interest lies in youth, and here his attachment to Oxford is paramount. Since his election to the Chancellorship in 1960 it has possibly done more to occupy his mind than any other single interest; and he has repaid the debt many times. What the pictorial record does not show is the already vast footage of files in the Birch Grove archives that deal with Oxford alone, in which the highly tuned address to the lesser college or humbler institution has always assumed a special precedence.

At Oxford there now hangs the latest portrait of Harold Macmillan, commissioned to celebrate the Chancellor's twentieth anniversary. A minor masterpiece by Bryan Organ (facing p. 174), it depicts a humorous, quizzical and somewhat roguish expression, and a certain ambiguity. You are not quite sure whether the subject is about to declaim on a matter of high seriousness – or whether a hilariously irreverent joke is in the making. In the course of my long sessions with him, I remember his once remarking on how important it was 'not to have a too rigid distinction between what's flippant and what is serious'. It was, I felt at the time, perhaps a key to an engagingly complex personality, as well as to his style of government.

Rather broad-mindedly, the only condition imposed on the official biography was that it should not appear during the principal's lifetime. As his ninetieth birthday approaches, which this pictorial biography is designed to celebrate, and his remarkable good health continues, however much I, like most authors, may enjoy seeing myself in print, I can only hope that the book on which I worked with Harold Macmillan for so long will not see the light of day for some few years to come. Meanwhile, the pages that follow serve as a vivid record of a fascinating life in our times.

ALISTAIR HORNE
*London*
*May 1983*

# A Solitary Child

'I do not feel bound to follow in the footsteps of any of my relations. I am here to act for myself. . . . The most important things must be done by myself – alone.'

These words were written in 1833 by the twenty-year-old Daniel Macmillan. They were to have a profound effect on his young grandson, Harold, almost seventy years later. Daniel, a Scottish crofter's son, surmounted poverty, illness and a lack of formal education to found – with the help of his brother Alexander – a publishing house which ultimately flourished. Their engraved portraits hung in Harold's nursery, and while still a child he read Thomas Hughes's biography of Daniel, warmed to his charm and strength of character and drew from him a romantic and heroic inspiration; the grandfather he never knew was the dominant figure of Harold's childhood. Throughout his life he has cherished a photograph of him set into another of the croft where he was born.

Through the hard work of Daniel and Alexander, consolidated and built on by their heirs, Harold was born (on 10 February 1894) into an upper-middle-class life, with a secure dynastic future available to him as a member of the prosperous and growing firm of Macmillan. Secretly, even in early adolescence, he had already decided to emulate his grandfather: he would place restrictive family expectations second to personal ambition. Daniel died in 1857 at the age of forty-four, only seven years after his marriage to Frances Orridge, a Cambridge chemist's daughter, and left behind him four children, including the four-year-old Maurice. They were brought up with their cousins by their uncle, Alexander, whose growing prosperity permitted him to send Maurice first to Uppingham and then to Christ's College, Cambridge, where he took a First in Classics. After some years teaching the subject at the academically distinguished St Paul's School, Maurice entered the family business to work alongside his uncle, his elder brother Frederick, and his cousin, George.

*While at Summerfields, my preparatory school in Oxford, before the rigours of the Eton Scholarship exam.*

1

He was reserved, taciturn, scholarly and influenced by the strong Christian Socialist tradition into which he had been born. Indeed, he was named after the movement's inspiration, his godfather F.D. Maurice, the author of the firm's first book and a moralist who sought unity in religion and its application to politics and society. Charles Kingsley, also a Christian Socialist and a bestselling Macmillan author, was the other godparent. Maurice Macmillan had portraits of both in his library, and though he kept his religious opinions to himself, his son was to say of him in old age: 'I know of no man who lived a life of greater unselfishness or rectitude.'

Maurice's choice of wife was unexpected – even exotic. Helen Artie (known as Nellie) Tarleton Belles was born in 1856 in Spencer, Indiana, to a doctor of Kentucky origins and his wife, née Reid, who was of Scottish descent. Nellie had artistic and musical talent, and when six months after her first marriage her musician husband (Mr Hill) died, she persuaded her parents to send her to Paris to study. After some years of modest success as a sculptor and singer, she met and married Maurice and settled down to being a model – though

*The remains of my great-grandfather's farm in the Isle of Arran.*

*My uncle Alexander, one of the founders of the firm, in the chair that my son still uses in the office.*

unusually strong-willed and energetic – Victorian wife, mother, hostess and philanthropist.

In her enjoyment of society and public activities, Nellie was in marked contrast to her shy husband. He was happy with a few intimates; she liked to fill the house (52 Cadogan Place) with her many artistic, literary and political friends and her colleagues from the committees of such organisations as the Women's Liberal Unionist Association and the Ladies' Working Guild. Yet, like Maurice, Nellie was serious minded and conscientious, and wanted her sons, Daniel, Arthur and Harold (who was christened Maurice Harold but always called by the second name to avoid confusion with his father) to grow up self-reliant, successful and honourable gentlemen. She was indeed intensely ambitious for them, providing every opportunity and encouragement as they acquired knowledge and excelled at their studies. As an aid to character-building, they were trained to austerity and self-discipline.

The Macmillans' notions of austerity were those of their period and class. Their tall, narrow house on the borders of Belgravia and Chelsea had an indoor staff of eight or nine, but Harold wore his

Above: *My mother in Indiana in the 1880s, and* (below) *later that decade in Paris, where she met my father. She was having voice training at the Conservatoire and clearly enjoyed* 'la vie bohème'.

brothers' cast-off clothes. Though Maurice was growing rich, there were no extravagant pleasures for the children. The chief recreation was reading and the chief excitements those publicly available. Among Harold's most vivid childhood memories were the celebration of the 1897 Diamond Jubilee – 'the endless procession of troops, of all races, with an infinite variety of uniform, led by Captain Ames, the tallest officer in the British Army' – and Victoria's funeral cortège four years later. More routine but infrequent even so were such treats as the Changing of the Guard, visits to the zoo, military bands in Hyde Park or hansom cab rides. Best of all were the railway journeys every summer, when the family, accompanied by four staff, went to Kent or Norfolk – travelling second class.

It was a childhood of order and certainty and Macmillan looks back on the nine-year reign of Edward VII with 'indulgent nostalgia'. 'For those of us who remember it,' he wrote seventy years later, 'the Edwardian summer was an Indian summer, the last "warm spell" of the Victorian Pax Britannica before the First World War engulfed us all and almost destroyed our generation.' Though the

*My brothers: Arthur, aged three, and Dan, aged seven, in 1893.*

*Myself at home, before I left for Summerfields.*

4

*My father, Maurice Crawford Macmillan, in 1882 at the age of twenty-nine.*

*1905, Summerfields school play. I was cast improbably as the Prime Minister, though the wig looks more like a Lord Chancellor's.*

belief that this world would last forever was unfounded, 'the peace and the sense of security which we enjoyed were not illusions. We really were at peace, we really did feel secure in the world.'

Harold was brought up mainly by his kind and fiercely patriotic nanny, Mrs Last. Daniel was eight years his senior, Arthur four, so for most of Harold's childhood he saw little of them, and had only occasional social contact with others of his own age until he went to preparatory school. He scarcely saw his father, and although his mother, by the standards of her class, took a close interest in him, she expected such high standards in terms of behaviour and study that he found her somewhat forbidding. Although he recognised later that but for her constant exhortation he would never have been an academic success, her demands weighed heavily on him. Even as a small boy, his failure to meet expectations in mental arithmetic was a sore trial to both of them. For all the security of his background, he was a sensitive, anxious and rather lonely child, fearful 'lest I might do something wrong or commit some solecism'.

When he was six or seven he was sent to Mr Gladstone's day-school in nearby Sloane Square, where he received a sound classical training before going on to Summerfields, in Oxford, in 1903. He

wrote of Summerfields' pupils sixty years later: 'whether we were happy or not, successful or not, scholars or not, athletes or not, we did somehow get into our heads that, if a thing was worth doing at all, it was worth doing as well as possible.'

He was a clever child, whose schoolwork was supplemented by tutors in the holidays and his own wide reading, which already encompassed a range from G.A. Henty and Conan Doyle to Dickens and Scott. He also had the advantage of fluent French, acquired from his mother and French governess and the domestic rule of speaking only French downstairs. It was no surprise when he won the Third Eton Scholarship of 1906. This achievement was slightly clouded for him by the knowledge that brother Daniel had won the First eight years earlier. In the same year his father bought a house and land in Sussex, next door to Lord Robert Cecil, who became a good friend of the family. Harold learned to love country things; they were to be 'a source of great happiness and relief' to him all his life.

Though he was reserved, Harold had already begun to make close, if not intimate, friendships, some of which lasted for life. That he could do so as a schoolboy was a tribute to his charm and intellectual distinction, for he was hampered in school life by ill health. At Summerfields he was considered delicate and was sent to bed before his peers. Soon after he went to Eton, he caught pneumonia and only just survived. And although he recovered enough to gain his solitary athletic distinction – playing for college at the Eton 'Wall Game' –

*The three Macmillan brothers at Cadogan Square: Arthur, to be an advocate; Daniel, a publisher; and Harold, a politician.*

*My grandfather, Daniel Macmillan (1813-1857), the joint founder of the publishing company in 1843.*

*The original Alexander Macmillan, my great-uncle. He was the brother of Daniel, my grandfather, and one of the founders of the firm. As he died in 1896 I have only the vaguest recollections of him, save that he frequently wore a sort of velvet smoking cap like a fez with a tassel.*

*My paternal grandmother, Mrs Daniel Macmillan, née Frances Orridge, who died in 1867; this sketch was done in Cambridge in 1850.*

*My maternal grandmother, Mrs J. Tarleton Belles, née Reid.*

he had to leave permanently in 1909, diagnosed as having a weak heart brought on by growing too fast.

It was hard to part – albeit temporarily – from friends for whom he felt affection – friends like Harry Crookshank and Henry Willink, both later to be Conservative Ministers, and Julian Lambart, later Vice-Provost of Eton. Harold had already discovered the joys of conversation and society that were to make him in later years such a clubbable man. Now he had to return to a solitary existence at home, relieved only by the permanent consolation of voracious reading, and the occasional stimulation of visits from tutors.

*The infamous Eton Wall Game: playing for College (the scholars) against the Oppidans (the fee-paying boys) in the autumn of 1911.*

In anything to do with education, his parents spared no expense, and Harold's tutors were of the highest calibre. His Eton tutor, A.B. Ramsay (later Henry Willink's predecessor as Master of Magdalene College, Cambridge) came to Cadogan Place once or twice a week to coach him in Classics, and they formed a close friendship that lasted until he died. Even closer was that which developed with a later Classics tutor, Ronald Knox, a Fellow of Trinity College, Oxford. Knox was only six years Harold's senior; he too had been to Summerfields and Eton. He had a splendid intellect and sharp wit that greatly attracted Harold, combined with a self-effacing manner and a deep spirituality that inspired affection.

Knox was at that period embarking on the journey that led him from Anglo-Catholicism to the Roman Catholic Church. He found Harold to be as much in need of spiritual guidance as of academic help. Harold, like his parents, was nominally Church of England. Nellie, who had been raised a Methodist, retained, in her son's words, 'strong Protestant feelings not to say prejudices', and she forbade Knox to talk with Harold about religion. Knox could not agree to this condition and, though he found it a 'horrid wrench', parted from the boy of whom he had become 'extremely (and not unreturnedly) fond'.

Their friendship could not be resumed until 1912, when Harold won an Exhibition to Balliol (where Daniel had been the Senior Classical Scholar). At eighteen he was at last free of the severe discipline of home or school. For him 'it was an intoxicating feeling to be on one's own, in a society of countless friends, old and new.'

Far left: *A. B. Ramsey, one of the masters at Eton who had a profound effect on my early schooldays. He was later Master of Magdalene, Cambridge, and then Vice-Chancellor.*

Left: *Daniel, my eldest brother, apparently as Bertie Wooster, 1912.*

Right: *Eton College Chapel at about the turn of the century.*

Below: *Fourth of June at Eton in 1907. With other Tugs – or scholars – in Weston's Yard for 'Absence', as roll-call is known at Eton. The white waistcoats were abolished in 1914 and the top hats in 1939 – victims of the two world wars.*

# Undergraduate and Soldier

Not only was Balliol, in Macmillan's view, 'the Mecca of the intellectual life of the world', it had also achieved notoriety for its policy of attracting students from a wide diversity of class and race. It provided an ideal environment for a young man seeking to expand his knowledge of the world while simultaneously stretching his mind and his talents.

Macmillan's academic work was guided by two brilliant Fellows, Cyril Bailey and Arthur Pickard-Cambridge, to whose help he attributes his First in Honour Moderations in June 1914. (He notes in his memoirs that his brother Daniel's First had been of a far higher standard but omits to mention that Daniel took a Second in his finals.) Apart from short trips abroad with friends, he applied himself to academic work during vacations – alone and in reading parties. In term-time he revelled in clubs, societies, convivial breakfasts, lunches and dinners, and all the manifestations of what he called 'an orgy of pleasurable social life'. Oxford also introduced him to the delights of alcohol – forbidden him at home.

Although he enjoyed comfort, he was no sybarite. Nor was there ever anything of the dilettante about him, for all that he cultivated the fashionable appearance of glorious amateurishness. He liked people who were witty and fun, but he was fundamentally serious and it was no accident that his friends were men of ability. Of those who survived the war, his Oxford friends included F.F. 'Sligger' Urquhart (a Balliol don), Humphrey Sumner (later Warden of All Souls), A.P. Herbert, Walter Monckton and Harry Crookshank, with whom he was now happily reunited. Above all, there was Ronald Knox, who became the dearest friend of all. In 1957, dying of cancer, Knox stayed with Macmillan at No. 10 Downing Street, and the Prime Minister saw him off at Paddington. It was only an example of one of Macmillan's most endearing qualities – his ability to remain constant to friends who had followed paths very different from his own.

*1915. I was lucky enough to obtain a commission in the Grenadier Guards.*

11

The intimacy with Knox ('the greatest wit and the greatest saint I have known in a long life') arose at Oxford from Macmillan's attempt to clarify his own religious position. Knox won him to Anglo-Catholicism. Macmillan served at his Masses, and with Knox's other chief disciple, Guy Lawrence, agonised about whether they should 'Pope'. They were seeking certainties from a man who was himself still undecided about whether to become a Roman Catholic convert, so although he drew great spiritual comfort from Knox, Macmillan postponed any serious decisions about future religious affiliations.

He had difficulties, too, in resolving his political ideas. 'My politics were confused. I was a Liberal-Radical, a Tory-Democrat, and a Fabian Socialist.' As if to prove the point he joined the Canning (a Tory club), the Russell (a Liberal one) and the Fabian society.

*Ronnie Knox, among my dearest friends at Oxford and throughout my life until he died in 1957.*

The confusion had much to do with his background. His much-admired grandfather had belonged to a social reforming movement that – though more religious than political – anticipated the Fabians. In later years the family became mainstream Liberal. They retained their admiration for Gladstone even after seceding to the Liberal Unionists after his conversion to Home Rule for Ireland in 1886. Maurice's friends ranged from the High Tory Lord Robert Cecil through the Liberal James Bryce to the Liberal-Radical John Morley. Nellie was more politically active in the Liberal-Unionist cause than her husband; but the Tory Arthur Balfour used to visit her at home and his sister Alice was a close friend. The only common factor among these political friends was their philosophical cast of mind.

There was a similar bewildering mixture among Macmillan's own friends. Although they included such orthodox Tories as Cecil's nephew, Bobbety Cranborne, others were mavericks like Herbert and heirs to the Liberal tradition like Cyril Asquith, whose father was very kind to Macmillan when he was brought to stay at Downing Street.

13

My brother Arthur when called to the Bar.

For two years Macmillan argued politics with these friends and at home with his brothers. (At last, in his late teens, he could meet Daniel, now a publisher, and Arthur, a lawyer, on more or less equal terms – a development that added greatly to the unity of the family.) As with corresponding arguments about economics, history, literature and religion, the variety of viewpoints he met enhanced his innate flexibility of mind and his capacity to fight his corner in debate. His reading now went beyond literature, and Disraeli was beginning to emerge as a profound influence on his political development and ambitions. 'If Dizzy had made himself leader of a party and Prime Minister by his own unaided effort, could not I have a go?'

Among the clubs and societies, pre-eminent was the Oxford Union. There Macmillan supported women's suffrage, the principles of socialism and the Liberal Government, and attacked the public schools for their inability to produce active citizens. He was cautious in waiting six months to make his first speech. Then, understanding from observation the nature of the audience, addressing a topic – the public schools – on which he felt strongly and having through the influence of the President, Walter Monckton, a position in the debate far higher than the usual tyro, he made what *Isis* described as 'a brilliant maiden speech'.

He gained recognition in the Union less as a debater than as an amusing and polished epigrammatist. His elegant figure and handsome face gave him a natural authority, and the hard work he put into his speeches left the harsh student reporters unable to find faults other than over-polishing, occasional inaudibility and a certain absence of original thought. His progress up the ladder of Union office was apparently effortless. Within eight months of his maiden speech he had been elected Secretary, and four months later, Treasurer. Had the war not put an abrupt end to his Oxford career, he would almost certainly have become President.

The Union offered Macmillan not only the opportunity to gain practice as a debater, but that of observing and learning from others. Of the mature speakers who came, he was most impressed by Lloyd George, whose 'fierce radicalism' and virtuosity at changing the mood of his speech and bringing his audience with him made Macmillan a life-long admirer. He could not hope to emulate that oratorical genius, but he could draw lessons.

Enchanted by '*la douceur de vivre*' – his own borrowing from Talleyrand's description of pre-revolutionary France – Macmillan spent the last few weeks of the 1914 summer term in the manner appropriate to a socially desirable undergraduate who had made his mark and was personally popular. When term ended he had plans for a reading-party with Knox, to be preceded by engagements in great

17

houses in London, where for the first time he was meeting female contemporaries. After one grand ball, on 28 June, he emerged in the early hours of the morning to hear a paperboy crying 'Murder of Archduke'. 'To me, as no doubt to nearly all my fellow-guests, this news had no particular implication.'

Within six weeks Britain had declared war on Germany, and Macmillan, recuperating from an appendectomy, was cursing his bad luck and fearing that he would miss a conflict generally expected to be over by Christmas. He was pleased when he was able to join the Artists' Rifles, whence – despite his poor eyesight – he was posted in the late autumn to Southend as a Second Lieutenant in the King's Royal Rifle Corps. He strove to master the technicalities of his new occupation, but was frustrated by his battalion's lack of professionalism (and even weapons) and by the fear that his was a regiment unlikely ever to be sent to fight.

His mother and certain Oxford friends came to his rescue. Through their influence he was given an interview with the Lieutenant-Colonel of the Grenadier Guards, a regiment whose marching had been a delight to him in childhood. He was accepted, and in March 1915 was gazetted to the Guards' Reserve Battalion. Like many others, he was seeking only the privilege 'of getting ourselves killed or wounded as soon as possible'.

That sense of untimely mortality drove his friend Guy Lawrence into the Catholic Church, where he expected Macmillan to follow him very soon. Macmillan lacked such impulsiveness, and concluding that, with his 'whole brain in a whirl', he was in no condition to take a step that would distress his family, he wrote to Knox that he was 'not going to "Pope" until after the war (if I'm still alive)'. Temperamentally, he preferred to set aside his religious and political doubts to concentrate on doing the best job his talents allowed, while seizing every opportunity to learn from the experiences he was about to undergo.

He trained at Chelsea Barracks and shared regimental pride in properly executed drill. For a few months he could live in Cadogan Place and meet in his leisure hours the many school and Oxford friends who passed through London. In July the Guards formed a 4th Battalion, for which he was selected, and in August it was sent to France. During the last week in September he saw his first action at the battle of Loos. He and his comrades gained a mile of ground at the expense of 45,000 casualties, among whom was Macmillan with an excruciating bullet wound in his right hand and a minor but painful head injury. In following orders with no apparent sense to them he first came to know 'what was meant by the phrase "the fog of war"'.

*A reading party from Oxford in Austria during the long vacation of 1913. I had already started smoking a pipe, a habit I fear that has never left me. I don't remember the name of the athletic man next to me wearing a Rowing Blue's jersey and cricket boots; I think he was killed in the First War.*

He spent almost three months in a hospital in London, based in the Lennox Gardens house of a friend of his mother's. Although his wounds healed fully, he was never to recover the full use of his right hand. In January he was posted to routine duties in the Reserve Battalion at Chelsea Barracks, and particularly enjoyed mounting King's Guard at St James's Palace. He again had time to make friends while he convalesced, and to mourn those who had already fallen.

Returning to France in April 1916, he was posted to the 2nd Battalion, where he was joined by Crookshank and other old friends. The battalion commander, Colonel C.R.C. de Crespigny, was a light-hearted, rebellious and fearless spirit who inspired Macmillan and his comrades in their dreary and frightening life in and around the Ypres Salient. Surrounding them were miles of seemingly empty battlefield in which, wrote Macmillan to his mother, were concealed trenches full of 'hundreds of thousands of men, planning against each other perpetually some device of death'. He was by now resigned to the absence of the glamour of old wars, and knew that battles came rarely. His tenacity withstood the test. In that same letter he wrote: 'We need not so much the gallantry of our fathers; we need (and in our army at any rate I think you will find it) that indomitable and patient determination which has saved England over and over again. If any one at home thinks or talks of peace, you can truthfully say that the army is weary enough of war but prepared to fight for another 50 years if necessary, until the final object is attained.'

Apart from severe concussion and minor facial wounds, he came away from Ypres unscathed. At the end of July, now a Captain, he left with the Guards Division to join the Battle of the Somme. In a preliminary action on 15 September he suffered a slight shrapnel wound in his right knee, but continued marching. Later the same day, after fairly heavy fighting, his battalion captured a line of trenches. While awaiting further orders, Macmillan took out a party of men to silence some annoying machine-gun fire on the left flank. The sortie was successful, but he was hit by machine-gun bullets which penetrated his left thigh just below the hip and lodged in his pelvis. Dazed but not in pain, he rolled into a large shell-hole.

He lay there all day between the captured trench and that which was his battalion's next objective. As the battle continued he phlegmatically read the book he carried with him – Aeschylus's *Prometheus* in Greek. As he remarked drily in his memoirs, it 'seemed not inappropriate to my position'. During counter-attacks he feigned death when German soldiers ran round his crater.

More than twelve hours after he was hit, a search-party carried him back to the captured trench. By now his left leg was useless and the shrapnel wound made his right no better. He was carried with another officer to Ginchy, where shelling was so heavy that they ordered the men to abandon them. Macmillan later observed that courage in battle was often motivated by vanity. Now, separated from his fellow-officer by darkness, he discovered extra physical resources through fear. Somehow he stumbled away from the bombardment, found a ditch and again lay there until rescuers arrived. From a dressing-station he was moved to hospital at Abbeville, where his wound began to heal without being drained. By the time he was despatched to England, inner abscesses had formed and his whole body was poisoned.

'I had had enough of being messed about by friend and foe,' he wrote years later. Exhausted and feverish, he summoned the willpower to persuade his ambulance driver to take him to Cadogan Place rather than to Essex. His mother found him a surgeon and a Belgrave Square hospital and an immediate operation saved his life. His condition was severe enough to keep him in hospital for much of the next two years. Though he won no decorations, according to a contemporary he inspired a Guards' saying – 'as brave as a Macmillan'. In great pain and consumed with misery as the list of dead friends grew remorselessly, Macmillan was back for the rest of the war to a solitary life of reading and reflection.

# New Departures

Once he was well enough to read again, Macmillan concentrated, though not exclusively, on history. He observed diligently the injunction of his hero, Disraeli: 'Read biography. There you have history without the theory.' Studying the lives of great men, following the military and political news, and pondering what he had learned from his war, he attained a clearer perception of his own life's objectives. Religion had ceased to worry him. He was now permanently secure in his adherence to High Anglicanism and he kept it apart from his politics which, though morally based, were pragmatic.

His soldiering had given him a great respect for discipline in civilian as well as military life. The performance of fellow-officers had taught him respect for the tolerance, generosity and breadth of vision of many who lacked academic background. Even more important, he had come to know and admire the steadfastness, humour and sentiment of the men he had led singing on their way to the horrors of trench warfare. Unlike his aristocratic friends, he had had virtually no contact before the war with members of the working class. Now he felt he understood and could get along with them, and he determined to devote his life to helping close the gap between the 'Two Nations'.

He was more confident, yet more humble, than before. The languid Oxford youth who found success in a narrow circle had become a man, who, though still rather shy and reserved, could recognise and respond to worthwhile qualities in all those with whom he came in contact. He now placed courage above all, and conceived a lasting contempt for those 'gentlemen in England now abed' who avoided active service – in either World War. In his memoirs he considers Simon Bolivar's division of mankind into 'gownsmen' (e.g., civil servants) and 'swordsmen' (men of action and leadership). He had been born and trained to the former condition; accident had led him to discover within himself some of the qualities of the latter.

*This spring day of 1920 on our return from Canada was undoubtedly the happiest day of my life.*

23

Politically, the fires of his youthful rebelliousness had been fanned by the generals well behind the lines who made bad decisions that sent millions to death. When Lloyd George toppled Asquith, Macmillan's sympathies were with the new Prime Minister – 'the rebel, the revolutionary' – who would not tolerate the mistakes of the High Command. Lloyd George failed him by authorising such disasters as Passchendaele, but Macmillan gave him due credit for being the architect of ultimate victory. He exempted Lloyd George from the bitterness he felt for the old men who directed the war, survived it and returned happily to their old political games.

Among his many dead school, Oxford and regimental friends, he was hardest hit by the loss of Guy Lawrence and Gilbert Talbot, ex-President of the Union and a young man of great political promise. Like so many of his generation, Macmillan was haunted by the memory of the dead: 'We certainly felt an obligation to make some decent use of the life that had been spared to us.' He and Sumner were the only survivors of the eight scholars and exhibitioners of their year. For a long time, Macmillan went rarely to Oxford, always with a 'strange sense of guilt' and only to visit his old and dear friends – Cyril Bailey, Knox, Sumner and Urquhart. Certainly there was no question of returning there to study after the war; there were too many ghosts.

Early in 1919, after a series of operations, his wound had healed sufficiently to make work possible. He was given light duties at Chelsea Barracks, while trying to find an escape route to a new environment with new faces. Although there was a place waiting in the family firm, he jumped at an offer to go to Bombay as ADC to the Governor, George Lloyd (later Lord Lloyd of Dolobran). His wound was still open and, to his deep chagrin, the doctors refused to declare him fit for India.

His formidable mother again solved the problem. Through her great friend, Lady Edward Cavendish, mother of the Governor-General of Canada, the Duke of Devonshire, she heard of vacancies on his staff for ADCs. Though Macmillan preferred India, he bowed to.the will of the doctors. In March 1919 he arrived in Ottawa.

He was there for only ten months – 'in many ways the happiest of my life'. His duties were not onerous, but opened up contacts with leading politicians, with several of whom – especially Mackenzie King, the Liberal leader, and Vincent Massey, an old Balliol acquaintance and later Governor-General – he formed friendships. At that period the role of the Governor-General was central to the relationship between Ottawa and London, and Macmillan encountered such burning political issues as the Canadian Government's demand for separate representation at the Peace Conference and the

right to appoint a Canadian Minister in Washington. It was his first exposure to the political changes that were rapidly taking place in the British Empire. Thus far he had felt romantic about its member nations and deeply grateful for the way they had rallied to Britain's defence. Now he began to appreciate that there could be no return to the pre-war status quo. This realisation was to make him unusual among Tory MPs during the 1920s, when he calmly accepted that the changes being brought about in dominion status were not only inevitable but desirable.

Macmillan was fortunate in the Governor-General he served. The Duke was a man of the kind to whom he naturally warmed – dignified, simple, wise and considerate. For his part, the Duke liked his young ADC and, having found him politically aware, discussed with him freely the problems that faced him. He had been a Minister in the Governments of Balfour and Asquith and he was a seasoned tutor

*The visit of the Prince of Wales to Ottawa in 1919. Dorothy is seated on the left at the front, next to her father the Duke of Devonshire, then Governor-General.*

*Social life in Canada was good. Right: Members of the Government House staff trying to net trout in a vivier in Blue Sea Lake. Below: Same group: left to right, Lord Haddington; Rachel Cavendish; Marion Cook (later Lady Minto); Dorothy Cook; Dorothy; and self; with Harry Cator 'at the net'. Dorothy's sister Blanche took the pictures. I don't recall if anyone fell in.*

Left: *The Fourth of June 1919 at Government House, Ottawa. Self with Harry Cator, one of the other ADCs; the hats would* not *have 'done' at Eton.* Above: *In the same year, Dorothy, her sister Rachel and the young ADCs: there seem to be a lot of legs in the picture. As we are in uniform, I suspect this was taken 'on tour' in the Provinces.*

*Bathing party: the Duke and Duchess with assorted daughters and ADCs.*

in practical politics and diplomacy. Macmillan also listened avidly to political gossip at Government House or over lunch at the Rideau Club, and attended Parliamentary debates whenever he could. His work brought the additional bonus of journeys around Canada, most notably to Quebec to welcome the Prince of Wales.

There was more to his life than politics. In London, even when out of hospital, Macmillan had been unable to join in the pursuit of superficial pleasure that kept many of his contemporaries sane. Reading and conversation with close friends like Osbert Sitwell were his only recreations. Now, in peacetime, he discovered again the joys of society. Government House was run like a cheerful house-party with constantly changing guests. During holidays there were fishing, boating, motoring and other diversions. It was a merry and healthy life, and contributed to the final healing of his wound, although the damaged bone was always to cause him pain.

Most magical of all his Canadian experiences was that of falling in love. Until then Macmillan had moved in almost unrelievedly masculine circles; he was ready to succumb to an attractive woman. Dorothy Cavendish, the Duke's third daughter, was pretty and un-sophisticated. She was nineteen to his twenty-five, and ill educated in the manner of her kind, but Macmillan did not expect of a woman the kind of intellectual companionship he sought from men. She was warm and sympathetic and within a few months they were engaged. Macmillan was set to join the vast network of the British aristocracy.

Their wedding at St Margaret's, Westminster, on 21 April 1920, was a very grand affair. The huge congregation boasted a bevy of royal and aristocratic guests on the bride's side, headed by Queen Alexandra, the Duke of York (later George VI) and the Duke of Connaught. The Macmillans matched the Devonshires in distinction if not in numbers by their convoy of literary giants, including three members of the Order of Merit – Lord Bryce, Lord Morley and Thomas Hardy. After a short period under the roof of Lady Edward Cavendish, the young couple moved to a house of their own in Chester Square, where Lady Dorothy bore four children – Maurice, Carol, Catherine and Sarah. She was a devoted mother, and for her husband a wise counsellor, who accepted philosophically the strains of marriage to an intensely ambitious man.

Although politics was his long-term goal, Macmillan was now happy to enter the family business in its old-fashioned premises in St Martin's Street. It had come a long way since 1843, when Daniel and Alexander – then Cambridge booksellers – had published their first book. Two years later Kingsley's *Westward Ho!* put them on the road to success, consolidated in 1857, the year of Daniel's death, by *Tom Brown's Schooldays*. Alexander showed great flair in development

The photographs taken after our wedding. A copy was sent to each member of the staff at both Macmillan and the Chatsworth estates who had contributed to our wedding presents.

A note from Thomas Hardy to my father congratulating him on the birth of his first grandson, my son Maurice. Hardy was one of the leading authors whom my mother invited to the wedding to 'balance' the Cavendish's royal and ducal guests.

MAX GATE,
DORCHESTER.

Jan 30: 1921

Dear Mrs Macmillan:

Congratulations to you & Mr Macmillan on the event in your son's household. I send this line to you & to them with a sense that I "assisted" at the wedding.

Always yours

Thomas Hardy.

Right: *Dorothy aged three, painted by William Carter.*

Overleaf: *My dear Dorothy, by de Laszlo, with the inscription 'My souvenir of your wedding, April 1920'. Ten years afterwards the artist did this portrait of me as a companion piece.*

and expansion, bringing to the firm in his lifetime worldwide fame as educational and literary publishers. *Macmillan's Magazine* included among its contributors Matthew Arnold, George Eliot, Henry James and R.L. Stevenson.

In 1920, the fortunes of the house of Macmillan still rode high under the leadership of Daniel's son Frederick, probably the most respected and personally popular publisher of his day. He had been the inspiration behind the 1900 Net Book Agreement that brought about the system of fixed retail prices. A founder of the Publishers' Association, he was twice its Chairman. His brother Maurice dealt with the overseas branches and concentrated at home on the educational side. Cousin George's contribution was mainly in the theology, classics and higher technical lists. Macmillan's brother Daniel and his cousin Will were junior members. Macmillan remembers the partners as true Victorians with a marked similarity to the Forsytes, who solemnly shook hands with one another every morning.

Sir Frederick was generous to his new apprentice and soon delegated to him responsibility for such senior authors as Hardy, Kipling and Hugh Walpole (with whom he formed an intimate friendship). In time he took on their glittering school of Irish authors – Yeats, George Russell ('AE'), James Stephens and Sean O'Casey, for whom Macmillan developed a great affection, believing that Communist and atheist though O'Casey claimed to be, he was, like Knox, a saintly man.

During the 1920s the elderly partners gradually handed over more and more work to the next generation. By the time all three died in 1936, the brothers were already in effect joint managing directors. They were good managers and businessmen, a sound if not – in publishing terms – brilliant team. Daniel's considerable academic intelligence earned him respect from authors of the calibre of his friend Keynes, but he was a nervous and shy man whose business relationships were often uneasy. Macmillan's charm, ease of manner and reliable if conservative literary judgement made him adept at handling authors, but his primary preoccupation from 1923 onwards was politics. His outside interests did, however, lead to a strengthening of the list in economics and politics.

In an era dominated by the innovatory genius of Victor Gollancz and Allen Lane, the brothers did not shine. Yet they kept the firm in family hands despite heavy death duties; they maintained its prosperity; the imprint remained one of distinction; and they did useful work in the Publishers' Association. They were loyally fond of each other, and Macmillan never ceased to be grateful to his brother for his kindness in encouraging him in a career that, from 1940, frequently forced him to relinquish entirely his publishing activities.

In Souvenir of 2nd Wedding
1920 April
de László

# Tory Rebel

Through intermarriage, the rich and powerful Cavendishes were connected with almost every great family in the land. Macmillan's mother-in-law, for instance, was the daughter of Lord Lansdowne, who had married a daughter of the Duke of Abercorn. One of Lady Dorothy's five sisters had married the Honourable James Stuart, a son of the Earl of Moray. Her eldest brother in 1923 married Lady Mary Cecil, the sister of Macmillan's friend Cranborne. Down the generations, the majority of marriages had been with aristocrats, with occasional infusions of new blood from the upper middle class. The Cavendishes might conceivably have reservations about Macmillan's involvement with trade, but they admired his intellect. Like them he was reticent and unassuming in personal relationships.

There was a timelessness about the Cavendish network and way of life that captivated Macmillan. Family Christmas at Chatsworth, the main house of his in-laws, meant – with guests and staff – the provision of food and shelter for about one hundred people. The reserved Duke and Duchess ('Granny Evie') were at their happiest surrounded by their many grandchildren, and loved to conduct the festivities according to nineteenth-century notions of hospitality.

Visits to Bowood, in Wiltshire, the seat of Lord Lansdowne ('Daddy Clan') and his wife ('Granny Maud'), were similarly redolent of the gracious past. Macmillan was touched by the ritual of the picnic, devised to entertain the ailing old man: the party would solemnly walk two or three hundred yards to a summer-house by the lake, where tables were laid as elaborately as in the dining-room and the normal luncheon was served by the butler and footmen.

Nor did the house-parties the Macmillans attended in other historic houses – such as Bolton Abbey (the Devonshires' August residence), Hatfield (the Cecils'), Cliveden (the Astors') and Wyngard (the Londonderry home near Stockton) – show any evidence that the war had much changed the lives of great landowners. Macmillan was more aware than his hosts that the days of such style were

*Birch Grove from the west. The house was rebuilt in 1926 on the site of an earlier building. It looks out over the Ouse Valley in Sussex towards the South Downs twenty miles away.*

numbered but, while it lasted, he took pleasure in the spacious luxury of his surroundings, the sense of continuity with previous generations, and the splendours of the architecture – for which his taste had been awakened at Eton and Oxford. He also learned to shoot, a pastime that was to be very important to him until, at eighty-four, his eyesight deteriorated too far.

He was not permanently dependent for his enjoyment of country things on the hospitality of new connections. Shooting was to become a feature of his life at Birch Grove, his parents' Sussex estate, where, in 1926, the modest home of his childhood was replaced by a substantial house ideal for relaxed family visits.

It was fortunate that the people with whom he now had close contact were worthy of his respect. Indeed, he admired many of them deeply. He had a great gift for seeing the virtues rather than the deficiencies of those with whom he associated, so he could form friendships with people of all parties, classes and nationalities. In many of his new relatives he found that uprightness, sense of duty, courage, modesty and decency that characterised the British aristocracy at its best. Many of them had gone unwillingly into the

*Dorothy, her mother Evy (Duchess of Devonshire), and her sister Rachel, later to marry the Hon. James Stuart, on their way to the Loder–Palmer wedding at St Margaret's, Westminster, in May 1922.*

*Shooting lunch at Meikleour, Perthshire, with J.J. and Violet Astor. Dorothy facing camera on the left in the cloche hat with the shiny band, self in the dark suit with both elbows on the grass. Others include: Mrs Mercer Nairn; Lady Cicely Vesey; Mr and Mrs Jeffrey Dawson; Diana Mitford; Captain McLeod; Captain Wedderburn; and Colonel and Mrs Edward Wyndham.*

*The pleasures of family life.*
*Right: Dorothy brings Sarah*
*home to Chester Square.*

Below: *My son Maurice aged two*
*with Daddy Clan, the Marquess*
*of Lansdowne, I think at*
*Bowood.*

Below right: *Bolton Abbey in the*
*Twenties. Self; Eve, the Duchess;*
*Duke Victor; unknown; and*
*Henry Hunloke and his wife*
*Anne, the Duke's younger*
*daughter.*

Left: *Maurice, aged two and a half, summer 1923.*

Above: *Christmas 1926 at Chatsworth. Maurice in front, then my niece Arbella Stuart and Andrew Cavendish, now the 11th Duke of Devonshire.*

*Maurice in 1924.* Below left: *at Westgate, and* (below) *with his pony at Chatsworth.*

field of politics, feeling themselves bound by the responsibility laid upon them by their great Whig tradition. Although he was of a retiring disposition, Lord Lansdowne had given fifty years of his life in the cause of public service. He had been Governor-General of Canada, Viceroy of India and Foreign Secretary. He had ended his career in public life amid bitter abuse over his proposals in 1917 for making peace with Germany.

The Duke of Devonshire was no less conscientious or brave. As Colonial Secretary in 1923, he declared that, when the interests of settlers and native inhabitants of a colony conflicted, those of the latter must be regarded as paramount. Traitorous in the eyes of many, the 'paramountcy' principle was to be of great use to his son-in-law many decades later.

With such notable examples before him, Macmillan could not contain his impatience to make his own mark. The Duke whetted his appetite during his two-year term of office by consulting him about political matters. His brother-in-law and good friend, Lord Hartington, was a Parliamentary candidate and some other contemporaries were already entering politics. When a General Election was announced for December 1923, he could not bear to remain simply an observer. Despite his admiration for Lloyd George, he realised

*My mother rebuilt Birch Grove in 1926, leaving almost nothing of this, the original house in which we had all been brought up.*

Birch Grove House.

*Chatsworth Christmas, 1928.*
*Back row, left to right: Ivan*
*Cobbold; self; James Stuart;*
*Eddie Hartington (later 10th*
*Duke); Anne Cavendish; Charles*
*Cavendish; and Evan Baillie.*

*Next row, left to right: Pamela*
*Cobbold; Maurice Macmillan;*
*Billy Burlington; Arbella*
*MacIntosh; and Andrew*
*Cavendish (present Duke).*

*Adults seated, left to right:*
*Blanche Cobbold, holding Patrick*
*Cobbold; Dorothy; Rachel Stuart;*
*Evy, my mother-in-law; Victor,*
*the 9th Duke, my father-in-law;*
*Dowager Lady Lansdowne;*
*Moucher Hartington, holding*
*Anne Cavendish; and Maud*
*Baillie, holding Peter Baillie.*

*Children, left to right: Jean*
*Cobbold; Catherine Macmillan;*
*John Stuart; David Stuart; Carol*
*Macmillan; Elizabeth Cavendish;*
*Judith Baillie; Michael Baillie.*

that there was no future for the Liberal Party, and that Labour could be fought only from within the ranks of the Conservatives – or Unionists, a term he preferred.

Having obtained leave of absence from the partners to fight an unwinnable seat for the sake of experience, he secured a candidacy by the simple expedient of going along to Conservative Central Office and asking. His background and connections eased his path. He was introduced the same day to the Chairman of the Stockton-on-Tees constituency party, who cheerfully offered him the nomination with a warning that it was by nature a Liberal-Radical seat.

Macmillan travelled to Stockton to fight his campaign, embarrassed by his innocence concerning constituency organisation or even what he calls 'the rough and tumble of the market-place and the street'. Fighting the election on the national platform of industrial protection, he was hampered by his abysmal ignorance of industry and Tees-side alike. Yet he was blessed with a quick sympathy for the unfortunate and by his great willingness to learn. It is a measure of Macmillan that in his first bewildering few days, he resisted pressure to sack his uneducated, illiterate Cockney agent. He quickly discovered the man's loyalty and efficiency and said after five elections that he 'never had a better friend'. And where another

candidate might have resented the statement from a devoted party-worker, Billy Ellis, 'You are no speaker: but you're a good lad', Macmillan was touched, and again he 'made a life-long friendship'.

Macmillan and Lady Dorothy learned together. As a canvasser she was 'natural, simple, and a little humble'. In over two decades in Stockton they built up a warm relationship with many constituents from even the meanest streets. Elections were 'jolly, rowdy and exciting' and he found he enjoyed the routine of electioneering, from the speeches in school-halls to the 'working men's clubs, smoking concerts, comic songs, women's tea-parties and outings'. He demonstrated early the combination of patrician manner, common touch and sense of fun that was to distinguish him throughout his life and earn him widespread personal popularity.

Much to his surprise, he lost by only seventy-three votes. Labour formed a Government that fell within a year, and in October 1924, at the age of thirty, Macmillan became an MP in a nationwide Tory landslide. 'For the first time in my life I heard the roar from thousands of throats, acclaiming victory.' In addition to his natural exhilaration, the new member felt a deep gratitude and sense of responsibility towards his constituents, which placed him firmly on that wing of the party preoccupied with the need to reduce unemployment and alleviate hardship. His visits to Stockton and the pathetic mail he received from desperate people encouraged him on a radical course that was to keep him out of office for many years.

In his memoirs he writes that perhaps his greatest gain from Stockton 'was the sympathy and humility that comes from understanding'. It gave him, too, a horror of unemployment that haunted him throughout his political life. There were those, including Attlee, who came to feel that the young Tory rebel's natural home was the Labour Party, but they showed in this a complete misunderstanding of the man. More than forty years after he first became an MP, he summed up the attitude that underlay his philosophy:

> . . . very often the transition from a few days at Stockton among my poor unemployed, to the various degrees of comfort and wealth which we all either commanded or enjoyed, left me with a growing sense of the great gulf. If much that was good and generous in the old way of life has passed away, it is comforting to reflect that these wide differences have been so largely closed in my lifetime. But the gap is surely better bridged by liberal and fertile acts of statesmanship to raise the level of the many, than by jealous and malicious policies that concentrate on pulling down the few.

The temper of the House of Commons during Baldwin's Prime Ministership of 1924–1929 was 'of modified but reasonable hope'. The League of Nations seemed to promise security abroad and there was a general confidence in the prospects for improving the lot of the people at home. Macmillan was able to defend Churchill's budget in his maiden speech on 30 April 1925 – an experience he found almost as frightening as 'going over the top'. He had deliberately waited for an unusually long period before first addressing the House. The care with which he selected his issue and the skill with which he planned his manner of speaking suggest that he had learned not just from watching others but from his beloved Trollope's account of how Phineas Finn met first disaster and then success.

Macmillan's speech was controversial in its attacks on the Opposition and thus brought him some notoriety. His content was

May I appeal to **YOU** to VOTE for my Husband.

I know that he will serve **YOU** faithfully and carry out all he has promised to do.
DOROTHY MACMILLAN.

*Despite Dorothy's and my efforts we tasted defeat in Stockton in '23, but we emerged triumphant in '24.*

# The Election Pictorial

## HOW UNEMPLOYMENT CAN BE CONQUERED —Page 2

*Incorporating*
### The LAND, MINING and INDUSTRIAL NEWS.

## VOTE LIBERAL —AND CONQUER UNEMPLOYMENT

# WE *CAN* CONQUER UNEMPLOYMENT

### UNEMPLOYMENT MUST BE CONQUERED

These pictures, showing the tragedy of unemployment, emphasise the urgent need for a sound policy—the Liberal policy, as outlined by Mr. Lloyd George—to prevent the continuance of this human misery. The pictures show:

(1) An unemployed man sleeping on the Thames Embankment.
(2) One of thousands of queues of despondent men waiting at an Employment Exchange for a job—or the dole.
(3) Children in an industrial area clamouring for food.
(4) A " soup queue " of unemployed outside a charity institution.

**The Liberal Party is pledged to remedy these evils, if you give it the chance (see pages 2, 3 and 8).**

40

impressive, but he had a great deal to learn as a Commons speaker. Lloyd George earned his permanent gratitude by instructing him in the tricks necessary in the House, about the need for light and shade and variation of both pace and pitch. His most important piece of advice was not to forget 'the value of the "pause"'. He would have been proud to see his pupil acclaimed as the master of timing.

Macmillan and Lloyd George became friends, the young man admiring the imaginativeness of the older's social and economic policies – most of them far more in line with Macmillan's thinking than those of the Baldwin Government. Within his own party he early acquired the reputation of a radical. He wrote articles calling for housing and rating reform and had the pleasure of being recognised by Churchill – with whom he had a happy informal relationship – as the inspiration of his decision to assist industry by relieving it of 75% of the rate burden.

*Lloyd George, probably the greatest orator of my time in politics. It was he who taught me the craft of making a Parliamentary speech. His theme does not seem unfamiliar.*

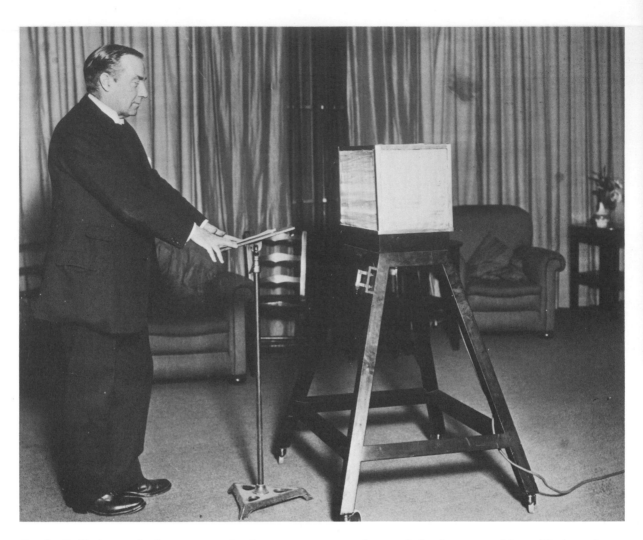

*Stanley Baldwin was the first Prime Minister to understand and use the new medium of broadcasting. It is remarkable how little the apparatus has changed over the years since 1924.*

Such successes were few and far between. Macmillan made no impact when he sought to persuade his leaders to act in a statesman-like and constructive way to ease the bitterness caused by the General Strike. Their failure to do so intensified his conviction that the Tory Party was blighted with the pre-war Liberal concept of *laissez-faire*. As part of a group of party left-wingers – popularly known as the YMCA ('Young Men's Christian Association') – he addressed himself to finding a constructive alternative to socialism, a quest that occupied him for the best part of ten years. With other members of the YMCA – Bob Boothby, John Loder and Oliver Stanley – he published in 1927 *Industry and the State*, a small book that sought to devise a system that lay between 'unadulterated private enterprise and collectivism'. It was privately praised by Neville Chamberlain and condemned by the right-wing press as 'thinly-veiled Socialism'.

Although in speeches and articles Macmillan always stressed the importance of progressive social reform and industrial reorganisation, during his first Parliament he was only gently critical of Government. Partly that was because he felt a young member should not be presumptuous; partly it was because, though they had not been inspired, the Government had been modestly reforming. Yet they had shown themselves unable to stem the growth of unemployment, which stood at 1.2 million when they went to the country in May 1929. Baldwin chose to fight the election on the dispiriting slogan, 'Safety First'. It awoke no enthusiasm among the Stockton unemployed, who voted Macmillan out: 'I had to confess, in my heart, that I could not blame them.' The right-wing press was delighted at the defeat of this and other 'semi-socialists'.

Although he had plenty to occupy him both as a publisher and as a newly elected Director of the Great Western Railway, Macmillan was not tempted to drop out of politics. He knew that Unionists must find a coherent approach to 'the modernisation of our economic methods, the humanisation of our industrial relations, and the expansion of our foreign and primarily of our imperial markets'. When Mosley resigned from the Labour Party in May 1930 over Govern-

*Stockton, 1929. Portable loudspeakers were infernal contraptions and always broke down at the critical point in a speech.*

## ELECTIONEERING UP-TO-DATE.

Capt. Harold Macmillan, the Conservative candidate for Stockton, addressing a street corner audience in Ewbank-street, through a microphone and loud speaker.

43

ment refusal to adopt his radical ideas, Macmillan defended him in a letter to *The Times*. Rab Butler was among those who recommended him to find 'a pastime more suited to his talents' than politics.

Macmillan flirted briefly with the idea of joining Mosley's New Party, but, rightly seeing no future for it, he decided to stay within his own and fight for his principles and his constituents. The Labour Party split in 1931 and Ramsay MacDonald (who in Macmillan's view had allowed himself to be intimidated by the Treasury and his Chancellor) formed a National Government to introduce the harsh measures deemed necessary to save the falling pound. A General Election was called while Macmillan was in a German clinic, taking treatment for a recurrence of great pain and lameness from his old wound, complicated by neurasthenia.

Above: *The Jarrow marchers affected public opinion considerably in the Thirties. Visits to my constituents in nearby Stockton* (right) *helped me understand their grievances.*

He returned to Stockton on two sticks in October 1931, regained his seat and came back to the Commons in fighting mood. There were now 2.7 million out of work, and he had no faith in the National Government's will to meet this challenge imaginatively. A trip to Russia in 1932 convinced him both of the value of state planning and the undesirability of totalitarianism. Capitalism, he was convinced, could not survive without radical change. Now very much under the influence of Keynes (a Macmillan author), over the next few years he and like-minded colleagues argued for a mixed economy, strategic state planning and intervention to bring about industrial reorganisation, modest reflation and a programme of public works. Fighting a long and thankless battle that effectively ruined his chances of office, he was motivated by his memory of the 'despairing faces' of the Stockton unemployed.

When Baldwin took over from MacDonald as Prime Minister in 1935, Macmillan fought the ensuing General Election on an independent campaign. He based his policies on a manifesto called *The Next Five Years* which he had partially drafted and which had the support of a wide range of public figures of all parties. Horrifying to orthodox Tories, it included recommendations for public control of transport, gas and electricity, nationalisation of the Bank of England, the abolition of the means test and an increase in death duties. On top of the many radical publications with which he had been associated in the early 1930s, this was calculated to put him finally beyond the pale of Tory respectability. For Macmillan, the taunts of 'socialism' were ironic. His abiding concern was to avoid a polarisation that would bring the country extreme socialism, by finding a compromise 'between the intolerable restriction of a totalitarian State and the unfettered abuse of freedom under the old liberalism'.

It was this theme that inspired the major book he began to write in 1936. *The Middle Way*, published in May 1938, called for urgent action to provide for all a decent standard of living by bringing the economic system under the direction of the State, and setting up a comprehensive scheme of national planning. Democracy, he said, could last only if it proved more efficient than socialism. What was necessary was a mixed system that combined state ownership or control of aspects of the economy with 'the drive and initiative of private enterprise'.

The intelligent, detailed and statistically based argument of the book was warmly received by the open-minded and, in the long term, proved highly influential within the party. In the short term it increased the suspicion in which he was held by the right-wing, who regarded him as an unmitigated nuisance. By now he was a rebel on foreign as well as domestic affairs. Up to the mid-1930s, he had

 **Daily**  **Express**

TO-DAY'S WEATHER: Fair.

NO. 9,790.    MONDAY, SEPTEMBER 21, 1931.    ONE PENNY.

# BRITAIN OFF THE GOLD STANDARD.

## LAST NIGHT'S DECISIONS BY THE GOVERNMENT

THE PRIME MINISTER running into 10, Downing-street on his return from Chequers last night for consultations in connection with the crisis.

| No More Gold To Be Sent Abroad. | Stock Exchange Closed To-day. | Bank Rate Up To Six Per Cent. |
| --- | --- | --- |

### BUSINESS AS USUAL.

### "THE INTERNAL POSITION OF THE COUNTRY IS SOUND."

THE GOVERNMENT announced last night that following the week-end demoralisation of the international money market:—

*The Gold Standard is suspended from this morning.*

*The Stock Exchange will not open to-day.*

*The export of money, except for bona-fide business, will be restricted.*

*A Bill to give effect to the suspension of the Gold Standard will come before Parliament to-day.*

Simultaneously the Bank rate is raised from 4½ to 6 per cent.

Provincial Stock Exchanges will follow the lead of London and close to-day.

The Chancellor of the Exchequer will broadcast an explanation of the position from all stations at 9.15 to-night.

### THE GOVERNMENT'S STATEMENT.

The following is the statement issued by the Government last night after a two-hour Cabinet meeting:—

HIS Majesty's Government have decided, after consulta-

citizens of foreign exchange (except those required for the actual needs of trade or for meeting existing contracts), and should further measures prove to be advisable His Majesty's Government will not hesitate to take them.

## GOOD NEWS.

THIS MORNING'S pronouncement from Whitehall is good news.

*Nothing more heartening has happened in years.*

Never mind how it came about.

Don't waste time in reviling the foreigner or in moaning about the humiliation of events.

*The fact remains that at last we are rid of the gold standard—rid of it for good and all.*

To future historians it will seem incredible that we should ever have been chained to an arbitrary metal, and that our financial standing in the world should have been at the mercy of unscrupulous and panic-stricken foreign investors.

Now our export trade will have its chance to grow, because the £ will be at its correct level and not an artificially sustained one.

It is true that for a time we shall have to purchase much of our foodstuffs from abroad ; but there is such a surplus of food commodities in the world, and since we are the one great importing country we shall be in the position to protect ourselves against excessive prices.

While we are doing this we can stimulate our own agriculture to the greatest degree, and, by taking our eyes away from New York, from Berlin, from Paris, we can go ahead with plans for a self-sustaining Empire.

*We repeat that whatever the difficulties and embarrassments of the moment, this morning's news is good.*

It is the end of the gold standard and the beginning of real recovery.

### DRAMATIC 'PHONE CALL TO CHEQUERS.

WHY THE PREMIER HURRIED TO LONDON.

FATEFUL MOVES.

FOREIGN ATTACKS ON THE POUND.

"Daily Express" Political

### FRANCE AND U.S. TO HELP THE POUND.

DISCUSSING CREDITS FOR BRITAIN.

"*Daily Express*" Correspondent.

WASHINGTON, Sunday, Sept. 20.

Franco-American co-operation to prevent the collapse of sterling will be forthcoming, it is believed in Government circles here.

The Federal Reserve Bank is considering further credits to Great Britain, and, it is understood, is discussing the situation with the Bank of France.

### MISS BONDFIELD ILL.

Miss Margaret Bondfield, Minister of Labour in the last Government, became suddenly ill during the week-end and was removed to a London nursing home.

She is suffering from a general nervous breakdown, caused by overwork.

Miss Bondfield is fifty-eight years old, and at the age of thirteen started work as a teacher in a board school.

### LATE NEWS.

*Sir Montague Norman, the far-sighted Governor of the Bank of England, brought Maynard Keynes into the financial establishment at a time when his policies were seen by many to be almost revolutionary.*

47

*Even in 1934 it was important for a politician to have what is now called the 'right image'. The charge of half a guinea for the rights to use this picture on an election address compares favourably with today's budget for electoral propaganda.*

BY APPOINTMENT

To

E

R 24/15/34

3873

Telephone: Welbeck 6855.

# ELLIOTT & FRY, Lᵗᴰ
## *Portrait Painters & Photographers*
### 63 BAKER STREET·PORTMAN SQUARE

Cheques crossed
"National Provincial Bank."

*London, W.1*    Oct 23ʳᵈ    1934

Harold Macmillan Esq M.P.

Messrs Macmillan & Co Ltd, St Martins St
WC2.

Folio

To fee for permission to reproduce
our portrait of
Self
for reproduction on political literature
for circulation in constituency

Our name to appear

10  6

supported the Government loyally on issues of which he was without specialist knowledge. From 1936, as he became aware of the drift and feebleness of its response to Mussolini and Hitler, he grew passionately concerned about foreign policy. He felt betrayed by Baldwin's failure to live up to his pre-election promises to resist Italian aggression in Abyssinia through the means of collective security, and in June 1936 took the serious step of entering with one other Tory the Opposition lobby in a vote of censure.

Although no action was taken against him, Macmillan felt it proper to resign the party whip. Baldwin's displeasure was evident in the brusque note with which he acknowledged the decision. Macmillan sat as an Independent Conservative for the rest of Baldwin's time in office, for he had wholly lost confidence in Baldwin's ability to handle important issues. Yet he wrote generously to express admiration for his skilful management of the constitutional crisis precipitated by Mrs Simpson. His letter ended with a rare manifestation of his religious views: 'The slightest weakness now would be a shattering blow to the whole basis of Christian morality, already gravely injured during recent years. May God help you at this painful and difficult time.'

Chamberlain took over as Prime Minister in May 1937 and Macmillan took the whip again. In February 1938, the Foreign Secretary, Anthony Eden, resigned with his Under-Secretary, Cranborne, in protest against being undermined by Chamberlain in the conduct of diplomacy. Macmillan was one of the twenty or so Conservatives who abstained in the vote of censure on the Government. Until the outbreak of war, he was a prominent member of the 'Eden Group' (or 'Glamour Boys') who ceaselessly criticised the appeasement policy. He also acted as a link with Churchill's followers and with sympathetic elements in the Labour Party.

For those whose eyes were open to the menace of Hitler, 1938 was a period of desperation. Macmillan abandoned his long and lonely campaign on industrial and economic policy to concentrate on trying to persuade the Government to stand up to Hitler before it was too late, by forming an alliance with France and Russia. His energy and tenacity were remarkable, for he had been brought very low by the deaths of the three senior partners and Rudyard Kipling in 1936, his mother in 1937, and the Duke of Devonshire in 1938.

In his private capacity he did what he could to alleviate the distress for which he blamed the weakness of Government. In memory of his father and grandfather he made a substantial donation to a social service centre in Stockton, and he gave shelter on the Birch Grove estate (which he had inherited) to forty or fifty mainly Jewish refugees. When the evacuation of London children started, the Mac-

*In 1940 we moved out of Birch Grove and made way for evacuee children from the Rachel Macmillan School in London. Being capable of reaching only three foot, they did much less damage than soldiers.*

millans handed over their house to a group of sixty or seventy and went to live in a cottage.

Although, like many anti-appeasers, he felt a momentary sense of relief over the Munich agreement, he swiftly realised its inevitable consequences. In October 1938 he savagely attacked the Government's foreign policy, abstaining over Munich and making eighteen public speeches on eleven consecutive days in denunciation of the agreement. In the Oxford by-election, he backed the Independent Progressive against the successful Conservative candidate, Quintin Hogg. To the distress of some of his Devonshire relatives, he placed an effigy of Chamberlain – complete with Homburg hat and rolled umbrella – on the Birch Grove bonfire on 5 November. His pamphlet, *The Price of Peace*, denounced Munich and called for rearmament and a British–French–Russian alliance.

Nothing he did had any effect. In consequence of his many years of stubborn independence, he was wholly without influence in a party governed by his intellectual inferiors. Nor did the various dissident groups of which he was a member have any more success. Hard to bear also was the ill feeling over Munich that made him socially objectionable to political opponents with whom he had till then happily consorted in his London clubs and in the Commons' smoking-room.

Macmillan found even more frustrating than his own impotence the refusal of the National Government to give any power to the two giants of the House of Commons – Churchill and Lloyd George. In a letter to *The Times* in March 1939, after Hitler had marched into Prague, he called vainly for a broad extension of the Government's political base. Miserably he watched the drift to disaster. Chamberlain's procrastination over the putative pact with Russia bore bitter fruit in the Molotov–Ribbentrop Pact of 22 August 1939. Ten days later, believing that the Anglo-French guarantee of Poland would probably not now be acted upon, Hitler invaded.

When Chamberlain finally declared war two days later, Macmillan left the House in a state of desolation, reflecting bitterly on the 'folly and blindness' of the official leadership of all three parties that had brought Britain to the catastrophe of another major war. He was a 45-year-old back-bencher with neither power nor influence. All his battles had been lost. He could feel none of the buoyancy and optimism of 1914. He could think only of the future that lay before his son, Maurice, a Balliol undergraduate of eighteen.

*My own children, all together at the outbreak of war, before we handed Birch Grove over to the young evacuees. Left to right: Catherine, Carol, Sarah and Maurice.*

# Administrator and Diplomat

'But what could I do? I was too old to fight. I had already tried to get back into the Reserve Battalion of my regiment; but they did not want officers of my age and physique. . . . I held no post. . . . Parliament did not seem likely to play a great role in the drama that was unfolding. The prospect, therefore, seemed flat and uninspiring.'

That mood did not last long. As Maurice abandoned Oxford to join the Army, Macmillan determined to fight relentlessly to ensure that his son's war would not be muddled through in the manner of his own.

As an MP, he had a double objective in speeches and behind the scenes: to influence Government in the direction of greater efficiency while doing everything possible to bring about a broadly based National Government under Churchill. In speeches he urged the swift introduction of controls, rationing, industrial planning and industrial mobilisation of the unemployed. With other dissidents he watched for opportunities to criticise Government for its obvious lack of decisive and imaginative leadership.

His first opportunity to see at first hand the Government's inadequacy came in consequence of the Russian invasion of Finland on 30 November 1939. He became a member of an aid committee and was delighted to be selected with Lord Davies as a delegate to Finland. He arrived there on 12 February, clad in a fur coat belonging to his brother-in-law, Devonshire, and a Swedish white fur hat (which he sported, with all the appearance of ingenuousness, on an official visit to Russia twenty years later). He saw in Finland a country 'struggling for its very life' without the help needed to sustain it. Having sent telegrams to the Prime Minister and Foreign Secretary begging for immediate aid, he returned to London 'obsessed by the Finnish tragedy'.

*With Anthony Eden, then Foreign Secretary, at Maison Blanche airfield in Algiers in 1943 after the allied landings in North Africa.*

53

*The Winter War. At the Finnish Embassy in Sweden in February 1940 with Lord David Davies, before going to Finland to support their struggle against the Soviets. The hat came in useful twenty years later.*

Finland fell on 13 March, having received from Britain only very meagre assistance. In the debate that followed Macmillan lambasted the Government for delay, vacillation and indecisiveness. Observing the front bench hostility to his searing criticisms, he could not have guessed that this would be his last speech as a back-bencher.

In April he joined a highly distinguished group of dissidents known as the Watching Committee. They failed to influence the conduct of the war but played an important role in marshalling opposition to the Government. Their opportunity came in May, when the House debated the events that had led to Britain being 'forestalled, surprised and outwitted' by the German invasion of Denmark and Norway. In close touch with Brendan Bracken throughout the debate, Macmillan was unsurprised when defections reduced the Government's majority from 240 to 81. Two days later Hitler invaded the Low Countries and Chamberlain resigned. To Macmillan's relief and delight, Churchill became Prime Minister on 10 May.

A couple of days later Macmillan was appointed Parliamentary Secretary to the Ministry of Supply. For a middle-aged man of outstanding intellect and energy, it was a humble enough post, but, untried in office, he was grateful for any opportunity to prove himself.

His greatest difficulty proved to be the psychological adjustment to intolerably long hours with few breaks for the genial and relaxed social intercourse that had for years been a constant delight. There were few opportunities now for agreeable interludes in his clubs – the Beefsteak, the Carlton, Pratt's and the Turf – or in the Commons' smoking-room. However, since he now had a small flat in Piccadilly, he was able to use any spare hours he had in making quick visits to his old haunts.

He had learned in the long years on the back benches how new Ministers tend to consider themselves a race apart, and he set an example of informality and friendliness in his dealings with those without office. To his workplace he brought in an unassuming way those social qualities that made him stimulating and fun to work with. It was typical of him that he rapidly formed with his raw twenty-one-year-old Private Secretary, John Wyndham, a friendship that kept the two of them in partnership for much of the rest of his political career.

*The King visits a bomber base in Lincolnshire during the early days of the war whilst I was still at the Ministry of Supply.*

He served three Ministers during his twenty months in this office: Herbert Morrison, Sir Andrew Duncan and Lord Beaverbrook. Morrison he found 'tough, imaginative and resilient', but out of his depth. Duncan was 'cautious, diligent, orderly, unimaginative, but efficient'. Beaverbrook 'radiated strength, authority, determination and energy' and was capable of cruelty and kindness alike.

In his highly effective contribution to the setting up of a system for the production of vital war supplies, Macmillan proved that he was a practical as well as a theoretical planner. In this, as in his other achievements in the Ministry, he showed that the years of studying and reflecting on the British economy and industry had been well spent. Although he was a strong believer in the need for discipline in wartime, he was no authoritarian. He did much to ease relations between Government, industry and labour and, as Chairman of the Industrial Capacity Committee, assisted in maximising output and eliminating production bottlenecks.

His talents as a planner and innovator and his mastery of detail were complemented by his skill in negotiation and his gift for inspiring his subordinates to work as punishingly hard as he did himself. From the time of Beaverbrook's arrival in June 1941, he had also the challenge of acting as the Ministry's spokesman in the Commons. He had to answer critical Parliamentary questions covering a range from departmental failure to provide reliable tanks to the alleged larceny of molasses. After thirteen years as a poacher, the new gamekeeper knew the tricks of mollifying critics, and his robustness, frankness and humour made him a formidable performer. Little did onlookers know that he suffered stage-fright that sometimes approached the point of nausea.

When he was moved on 5 February 1942 to the post of Under-Secretary of State for the Colonies, he received an unusual accolade for a junior Minister – membership of the Privy Council. Churchill had deliberately transferred him to a job where he was working for a peer. When Lord Moyne was moved after three weeks, Macmillan was delighted that his successor was his old friend Lord Cranborne: 'No man could have wished for a more delightful or generous chief.' They shared common attitudes and Cranborne delegated to Macmillan full responsibility for economic and trade issues.

As he began to appreciate the importance of the department and the ability of its staff Macmillan revised his initial opinion that he had exchanged a madhouse for a mausoleum. The Colonial Office dealt with fifty-five colonies and sixty million people. Its primary task was to mobilise all the resources of the Empire. With shipping under constant threat the importance of rationalising imports and exports was vital to the success of the war effort.

During Macmillan's tenure of office Britain fought frantically for survival. Defeat followed defeat and not until October 1942, with El Alamein, did the tide begin to turn. In such circumstances, Macmillan had to concentrate on short-term problems. He put his position bluntly in June 1942, when 'unhesitatingly' defending the application of industrial conscription measures to the colonial population 'on the only ground on which they can be defended – the overwhelming, insatiable, devouring demands of war'.

As far as the post-war Empire was concerned, he foresaw a great development in the principle of partnership, but with little time to give to other than urgent matters, it was not surprising that at that moment he failed to anticipate the speed and fundamental nature of post-war colonial change.

His contacts in and experience of the Ministry of Supply added to his effectiveness in his new job, but his enjoyment of it came to an abrupt end in late November when his old YMCA friend, Oliver Stanley, took over as Minister. Stanley's reforming zeal had not kept him from office and there had been some strain between them after Munich. They liked each other, but Stanley seemed neither decisive nor willing to delegate, and he took over Macmillan's Commons responsibilities. In his frustration Macmillan drafted a letter of resignation which Bracken persuaded him to delay sending to Churchill. It was wise advice. Just over a month later, on 31 December 1942, Macmillan and the faithful Wyndham were *en route* to Algiers, where he had been appointed Minister of State in North Africa with Cabinet rank.

The job in which he was to make his reputation as a heavyweight had to be built up from nothing. He was to work at Allied Forces Headquarters (AFHQ) as a channel of communication between Churchill and the Supreme Allied Commander, General Eisenhower. Although land, sea and air forces were all under the British command respectively of Alexander, Cunningham and Tedder, AFHQ was staffed equally by both nationalities. Churchill had explained frankly that success in the job depended on the influence Macmillan could wield, but that it was a post at the centre of world events and 'an adventure of a high order'. Macmillan had accepted with alacrity.

During the wilderness years he had found himself intellectually superior to the mediocrities who dominated successive Governments; his judgement had been proved accurate by events; and experience of office had polished his propensity for influencing and getting the best out of others. 'I *know* I can do it,' he once said to Wyndham with great force. And thus he confidently staked his future on a gamble.

*Wartime Algiers saw many famous visitors. Left: 'General Lyon': the arrival of the King in Algiers in 1943. Left to right: self; A.B.C. [Admiral Cunningham]; Air Marshal Tedder; and General Eisenhower. Below: Field Marshal Smuts arriving at Maison Blanche airfield in 1942. He was under constant pressure from the Boer anti-British lobby to keep South Africa out of the conflict as far as possible.*

Algiers, 1943. A covey of present
and future Prime Ministers face
the press.

Arriving at the villa in
Casablanca with Winston,
January 1943.

*Waiting for our lords and masters:*
*Sholto Douglas; self; Bedell*
*Smith; and Bob Murphy.*

Calling on Eisenhower shortly after his arrival in Algiers, he was met with a courteous but discouraging 'Pleased to see you, but what have you come for?'. Macmillan turned a potentially disastrous meeting into a success by casually mentioning his mother's Indiana background. An hour later the General had told him openly about the political problems that bedevilled him.

Almost as crucial as Eisenhower to the success of Macmillan's mission was his personal political adviser, Robert Murphy. Macmillan already knew enough of the politics of North Africa to realise that there was on many issues a vast gulf between the British and their American allies. As Murphy was distrusted by the British so Macmillan was initially distrusted by the Americans. Within a few days of their first rather uneasy meeting, their excellent working relationship and life-long friendship had begun on a basis of mutual frankness. Macmillan had won Murphy's confidence as he was to win that of his colleagues – by listening rather than talking and by striving to understand his point of view.

Wyndham was soon writing home: 'Uncle Harold is being a great success. He is much liked, his sincerity is admired, and he has made constructive suggestions which have been hungrily welcomed.' It was no exaggeration. Macmillan had disarmed hostility not just by his engaging manner, but because it was obvious that he genuinely admired and liked Americans. The ties of kinship had always mattered to him; he had never forgotten the relief he felt when America entered the First World War; and before they even entered the Second, he had given them credit for saving Britain from certain disaster by the introduction of Lend-Lease. Seeing him as a trustworthy ally, his American associates – and Murphy in particular – worked with him to minimise, not magnify, the differences of view held by their respective principals.

The major political problem in North Africa was to find a French leader who could win over the French colonies to the Allies. The United States favoured the agreeable, inept General Giraud; Britain backed the touchy, demanding but inspired leader of the Free French, General de Gaulle. At a secret conference in Casablanca in late January, attended by Churchill and Roosevelt, it was decided to effect a shotgun wedding between the two Frenchmen.

Both were invited to attend and de Gaulle, gripped by his usual excess of *amour-propre*, came reluctantly and tardily. His inflexibility throughout the negotiations angered Roosevelt and almost lost him Churchill's support (and earned him at AFHQ the sobriquet 'Ramrod' – all the rigidity of a poker without the occasional warmth). It was owing to Macmillan and Murphy that de Gaulle was not jettisoned. Tireless diplomacy produced an appearance of unity between the generals and gave Macmillan time to strengthen the case for de Gaulle. He believed him to be the only man who could rally the French in North Africa and bring stability to post-war France.

Macmillan's new career almost ended in late February. He was to go to Cairo and persuade Admiral Godfroy 'by guile or force' to surrender the French fleet to the Allies. The plane crashed in flames during take-off and Macmillan was trapped. He struggled desperately over a mass of jagged obstacles and climbed out of the pilot's side-window just before the plane exploded. Once again, he recorded, fear had been the spur. His legs were cut and his face badly burned. One of his co-passengers, a French Admiral, bewailed the loss of his cap: '*Ma casquette*; *ma casquette*! *J'ai perdu ma casquette.*' Macmillan was heard to retort, 'I don't care a damn about your *casquette*. *J'ai perdu my bloody face.*'

Below left: *Algiers, 1943. Left to right sitting: General Catroux; de Gaulle; Winston; Giraud and Anthony [Eden]. Left to right standing: Jean Monnet; Philip; self; Georges; Alan Brooke; A.B.C. [Admiral Cunningham]; and René Massigli.*

Between burns, severe shock and concussion, he was out of action for over two weeks. He set off for Cairo again on 6 March and undertook the lengthy negotiations that ultimately led to the surrender of the fleet. His proven physical and mental resilience enhanced his growing reputation for what was to become known as 'unflappability'.

In July, largely owing to Macmillan's patient work, Britain and America recognised de Gaulle as *de facto* Prime Minister of the French Provisional Government. Macmillan had overcome the prejudices of the Americans, the irritation of London and the frequently impossible behaviour of de Gaulle himself, by exercising his fundamental strategy as a political adviser: he was influential because he appeared to have no ambitions to influence; powerful because he showed no apparent interest in power. He was adept at giving credit to others and at making them believe they had generated the ideas he put into their heads. His fluent French, understanding of the French character and the natural sensitivity that

*With Duff Cooper in 1944, shortly before his appointment as British Ambassador to the newly liberated Paris.*

*Previous page: The Cairo Conference, 1943. A most extraordinary performance and, I suppose, a useful one. Seated left to right: Generalissimo Chiang Kai-Shek; F.D.R.; Winston and Madam Chiang. Standing left to right: Cadogan; unidentified; Anthony; Steinhardt; John G. Winant, US Ambassador in London; self; Dr Wong Chung-Hui, Secretary General of the Chinese Defence Council; Dick Casey, British Minister in the Middle East; Lord Killearn, British Ambassador in Cairo; Alexander Kirk, US Minister in Cairo; Averell Harriman; Douglas; two unidentified; and Hopkins, special assistant to F.D.R.*

helped him appreciate the defensiveness of a defeated nation were powerful weapons. He never sought concessions from de Gaulle; he secured them through Frenchmen who trusted him – among whom General Catroux, René Massigli and Jean Monnet gave vital help at the critical times.

Until the beginning of 1944, when Duff Cooper was appointed Ambassador to the French Provisional Government, Macmillan continued to play a vital role in ironing out Anglo-American–French differences over the running of the French colonies. His task had become much easier as he built a friendship with Eisenhower and mutual respect with de Gaulle.

French affairs were by no means his sole concern. From February, when the Allies took Tunisia, plans were in train for an invasion of Sicily as a first step to the Italian mainland. As Macmillan grew close to Alexander as well as Eisenhower, he found himself drawn into discussions on political implications. In June Churchill formally made him political adviser on Italy.

For much of 1943 Macmillan commuted between Algiers and Tunis; he made occasional trips to London; he accompanied the King from Algiers to Malta in June; in August, after Sicily was won, he accepted Alexander's invitation to Syracuse; in September, with Murphy, he went to southern Italy, now in Allied hands, to meet King Victor Emmanuel and Prince Umberto; in November he flew to Gibraltar to meet Churchill on HMS *Renown*; and he was in attendance at the Cairo conference later that month.

*Awaiting Winston's arrival in Casablanca in January 1943 with Alex, for me undoubtedly the greatest commander of the Second War, and* (below) *with Alex in Italy.*

Most of his journeys were accomplished in unpressurised, freezing aircraft (he found Boswell suitable reading on such occasions), and wherever he went he was involved in delicate negotiations with military and political figures of a rank far higher than his own. In October he succumbed to a high fever and at the end of the year developed troubling and prolonged eczema. He was forced to take four weeks' leave in England, interrupted by talks with Churchill and the Foreign Office. Yet for the most part he survived unscathed, bolstered by a sound constitution, fascination with his work, and delight in danger and challenge.

From January 1943 he was vaguely briefed to report to Eisenhower's successor in the Mediterranean, General Wilson, on all countries under his control except Turkey. Macmillan carved out a position acknowledged by historians to have been one of colossal power. As Wyndham put it, he became 'Viceroy of the Mediterranean by stealth'.

Five major problems occupied his attention during the next sixteen months. First was Italy. Was she to be treated as a friend or foe and should she (as Britain wanted) remain a monarchy, or (as America wanted) become a republic? Macmillan believed strongly

*The liberation of Modena in Northern Italy, late summer 1944. The Italian crowd seems more pleased to see the photographers than to see the British Minister.*

The victors: in Italy, May 1945.
With General Mark Clark,
commander of the American
forces, at his headquarters, and
with the inevitable public relations
man, Mr Stewart Brown.

that she should be treated as a friend and had already been of considerable influence in securing generous surrender terms and giving
priority to feeding the starving population. He was to have an even
more crucial influence in ensuring the the Advisory Council for Italy
(on which he was UK representative) settled for indirect control of
liberated Italy. As Acting President of the Allied Commission from
August 1944 he made considerable progress in sorting out the
country's economic and political chaos preparatory to self-
government.

Where the monarchy was concerned, he was only temporarily
successful. Although he engineered a compromise between the King
and the Americans – a transfer of power to the Prince when Rome
fell in June 1944 – the monarchical principle had been fatally undermined. Umberto finally became King in May 1946: the following
month the electorate voted for a republic.

The second problem concerned the next stage in the invasion of Europe. The Americans were committed to 'Operation Anvil', the invasion of the south of France. Alexander convinced Macmillan that an attack on Austria, the 'soft under-belly' of Europe, was preferable. Such a strategy would have placed the occupying forces in a position of strength in the Balkans. Macmillan fought hard in London in June 1944 for Alexander's 'Operation Armpit', but though Churchill approved it, the Americans were immovable. It was to be a matter of great grief to Macmillan when the Balkans fell under the hegemony of the Soviet Union without a struggle.

The third preoccupation was Yugoslavia, where the Americans were sympathetic to the monarchist partisans while the British realistically backed the far more effective and popular Communists under Tito. Macmillan was a major force in months of talks from the summer of 1944 that brought about a measure of unity between monarchists and Communists. His primary achievement was to defuse American anger at British support for Tito. The Yugoslavian leaders accepted a settlement that promised democracy. That totalitarianism was imposed in November 1945 was an indirect consequence of the rejection of 'Operation Armpit'.

Greece was the fourth concern. Macmillan had to work hard to convince Churchill – a committed Greek royalist – that a Communist take-over could be avoided only by compromise with moderate republicans. After talks at Caserta, now AFHQ, Macmillan sailed in mid-October to Athens with the British liberating fleet that restored the exiled Greek Government under Papandreou. During October and November, he commuted between Caserta and Athens, working to solve the country's economic problems and disarm the Communist partisans.

He was in London in early December when the Greek civil war broke out. Churchill's support for Papandreou was under heavy criticism from the neutral Americans, and the British left. A magnificent speech rallied Commons' support, whereupon he sent Alexander and Macmillan to Athens to try to restore stability.

They arrived on 11 December and what Wyndham called 'the firm of Macmillan's Mediterranean and Balkan Salvage Enterprise' found itself besieged in an overcrowded British Embassy by snipers. They spent three weeks there in primitive conditions.

Through persistence and firmness – and with the help of a visit by Churchill and Eden at the end of December – the moderate forces were brought to unite around Archbishop Damaskinos as Regent; a peace settlement was agreed with the Communists. Churchill and Eden returned from Yalta on 14 February 1945 to be cheered by large crowds. The importance of Macmillan's contribution can be

*The famous visit by Churchill in December 1944 to Athens, perched on the brink of civil war. Winston is seen walking with Archbishop Damaskinos. I am with Anthony Eden and on the right of the picture is the Embassy information officer, Osbert Lancaster.*

gauged from a letter Damaskinos wrote to him later, in which he said: 'Your penetrating intelligence, your devotion to my country, and the friendship you have shown me since then, have been of invaluable assistance in the difficult path I have had to follow.'

Finally, Macmillan was involved in the decision that caused him much heart-searching but to which he saw no alternative – the repatriation of about 40,000 Cossacks and White Russians who had been taken prisoner by the Germans earlier in the war.

Macmillan gave up his post on 26 May 1945, after almost two and a half years as Minister Resident. From inauspicious beginnings he had reached a position of power that had him in control of four ambassadors. He had achieved in Britain, America and the Mediterranean a reputation at top level for high intellectual ability, shrewd political judgement and diplomatic gifts well beyond the norm. He had helped restore stability to the Mediterranean and had played a vital role in maintaining harmonious Anglo-American relations.

e would ... r. Peat de- t stage to would be eat again

about 40 ddressed in immediately on, Mr. Peat shall have to ce hard times times—during years, and I these years country will reciate and

TION"

we shall in three think that ill see West- 5 years." the market a crowd of eople, Coun. ow this great place people leaders and ive a great onstruction. nternational themselves, ill lend a with her he recon- d Europe. ous prob- Govern- age, those ed, as they by Labour countries. better the for the whatever ver their

F TION

Reason re

..... 12,024 8,600

It looks ... ke a fair cop ... ... ... out the squad of police are only escorting their M.P., Mr. Alec Spearman, Conservative from the Town Hall.

## Stockton

# EARLY RESULT GAVE ONE OF FIRST SURPRISES

## Mr. Harold Macmillan Defeated by 8,664 Majority

G. R. Chetwynd (Lab.) 27,128
M. H. Macmillan (Con.) 18,464
G. P. Evans (Lib.) ...... 3,718

LAB. GAIN. Maj. 8,664
1935—Macmillan (Con.) 23,285, Miss Lawrence (Lab.) 19,216; Tossell (Lib.) 5,158. Con. maj. 4,068.

This was one of the earliest results declared, the time being 9.50 in the Corporation Hall, where the counting took place, or 50 minutes after it began.

Mr. and Lady Dorothy Macmillan arrived just as the result was declared. Mr. Macmillan had come by train from London.

The result comprised one of the first surprises of the election. It was declared from the Town Hall at 10.5 by the Mayor (Coun. A. Ross) and, not having been expected so early, there was only a small crowd present. The candidates, Mayor and Town Clerk (Mr. Eric Bellingham) walked to the Town Hall from the Corporation Hall in West-row.

Capt. Chetwynd in moving the vote of thanks to the Mayor as returning officer, said that he hoped Stockton had given a lead to the rest of the country

and there would be a Labour Government in power.

Mr. Macmillan, in seconding, congratulated Capt. Chetwynd and said that he knew that he would distinguish himself in the House of Commons. He added that it was his sixth contest of Stockton and he had won three and lost on the other three occasions.

### DEPOSIT FORFEITED

Mr. Gordon Evans, who loses his deposit, observed that the election, by the clean way in which it had been fought, had upheld the best traditions of British democracy.

Later Capt. Chetwynd, M.P., told the Northern Echo: "This election has been won because we have appealed to the electorate on a policy and not on personalities. This election has proved that thinking people refuse to be stampeded by election scares. The enthusiasm shown by all for the Labour cause has reaped a great reward. I assure the people of Stockton that I will serve them to the utmost of my ability as their representative."

There were 82 spoilt voting papers and the percentage of those voting was 80.

count which duced onl tions in th When the to a crowd Municipal Jones said: day in the Labour party "We have t won the seat, a has happened bolical of what and down the a triumph people"

"WILL FI Col. Green congratulate heartily on "Coun. well that dead in th will certain again." The Lib G. Russell do sincere first Labo Hartlepoo. that every constituenc party, will what Labo native tow Mr. Ha Independen deposit, ad tions and s the short p duct the satisfied w had receive Contrary proportion fell to 76. with 83.1 pe number w exceeded 12 tive poll fell to 16,227, w in favour o Labour cand cally unchan

Spennymo

FEW PE

Co.der

## Scarborough and Whitby

**LABOUR VOTE ALMOST T...**

## Bishop Auckland

**MR. DALTON ON TORY**

There had been occasional criticism at home. Churchill had thought him too pro-French; Bracken believed him unduly pro-American; Sir Alan Brooke objected to his involvement in securing Wilson's replacement by Alexander in November 1944. These were passing irritations and his contribution was applauded in the higher echelons of Government. He had proved resourceful beyond all expectations and could never again be overlooked for office.

When he returned to London he became Secretary of State for Air in the caretaker Government between the resignation of the National Government and the declaration of the General Election results on 26 July. He found himself almost entirely out of touch with domestic issues and felt 'a flatness and frustration' in his new job.

Compared to his London-based Cabinet colleagues, he was virtually unknown in the country. Through loyalty to Stockton, he had turned down a safe seat. But he had been able to visit his constituency only once since 1942 and was not surprised when he was heavily defeated in the landslide Labour victory. He now had to consider seriously whether he wished to continue in politics.

*The* Northern Echo *report of the defeat in the great Labour landslide of 1945, which sadly marked the end of my long and happy association with Stockton.*

# Opposition and Office

Consideration for the firm and the family, with both of which he had long been largely out of touch, briefly tempted Macmillan to retire from public life. Maurice had married Catherine Ormsby Gore (Cranborne's niece) in 1942 and Macmillan was now a grandfather. It would be pleasant to savour at leisure the delights of family life and to give up the frustrations of politics without power. But Britain must surmount the war's devastation of her finances, industry and markets, and the challenge could not be ignored. Churchill, at seventy, was cheerfully looking forward to leading a future Conservative Government, and ridiculed the 51-year-old's hesitancy. He was nominated for a safe seat in Bromley where a by-election was imminent.

Macmillan and Lady Dorothy always missed Stockton and found it difficult at first to adjust to a prosperous southern constituency, but there was a warmly auspicious start to his happy nineteen years as Bromley's MP. He campaigned defiantly on the principles of *The Middle Way* and won a comfortable majority.

He returned to the House on 20 November 1945, introduced by Crookshank and Willink, two contemporary Eton scholars, and was appointed to the fourteen-man Shadow Cabinet. Its members had no specific portfolios, and Macmillan, facing a Government majority of 180, found comfort in the scope he was given to tackle any issue that appealed.

The Shadow Cabinet included two relatives by marriage – Salisbury (Cranborne had succeeded as Marquess) and James Stuart – and a number of old friends, including Crookshank and Oliver Stanley. R.A. Butler was one of its rising stars, but there was no sense of competition, for Churchill was unchallenged as leader and Anthony Eden as heir apparent.

*My tenure of the Foreign Office was all too brief before Anthony Eden, one of our greatest Foreign Secretaries, moved me on to the Treasury. I had often dreamed of sitting in this room, and I finally realised it in 1955.*

*Back to Westminster. With Winston during the by-election at Bromley in 1945.*

Macmillan, with Butler, Oliver Lyttleton and Stanley, tended to concentrate on economic and financial issues. As the Government embarked on its massive programme of nationalisation and social reform, he often found himself in embarrassing agreement with their principles; Bracken spoke for many on the Tory right when he privately described Macmillan as a 'neo-socialist'. Furthermore, he felt genuine admiration and affection for many on the opposite bench. In his memoirs he writes glowingly of the abilities and personal virtues of Attlee, Bevan, Bevin, Cripps, Dalton and Morrison. Smoking-room arguments with his opponents, most notably with Nye Bevan, were occasions he relished.

His solution was to exploit without quarter the differences that did exist: he criticised the headlong speed and projected scope of nationalisation, the damage caused by the restrictive practices of employers and unions, the Government's insufficiently expansionist economic policies, and Cripps's draconian austerity measures. His party loved his forceful and hard-hitting delivery, though opponents considered his style mannered, his Edwardian elegance a pose and (echoes of the Oxford Union) his speeches over-polished. Macmillan was later to agree that he had over-prepared his speeches in Opposition and indulged too much in paradox and epigram. More serious was the accusation of cynicism: that he was attacking a Government philosophically closer to him than his own.

This was an unfair jibe. Although Macmillan undoubtedly took a partisan line, he did not modify the attitudes of his youth. He sought instead to gain their acceptance by the Conservative Party. During 1946 he launched a crusade to force an internal party debate on its principles and its policy. At rallies and fêtes he spoke of the need to modernise the party, for when the reaction against Labour came, 'we must be armed with the spiritual weapons of unity and faith. The new democratic party – for that is what it will be – must be prepared for its high task.'

He even pressed for a Liberal–Conservative merger and the adoption of a new name. He had always disliked the overtones of the title 'Conservative' and preferred to call himself a Unionist – 'representing unity of the Empire, the essential unity between the Crown, the Government, and the people', and implying a dislike of class conflict. The Liberals were unconvinced, and there was no support for changing the party name, yet Macmillan's crusade was conspicuously successful. It was in no small measure due to him that the party conference in October 1946 demanded a restatement of Conservative policy in general, and industrial policy in particular.

*The years in opposition laid the foundations for the 'Thirteen years of Tory misrule', but the European question never received the full support of the Party. In October 1949 I wound up the debate on Europe at the Party Conference in London.*

A committee on industrial policy was set up with Lyttleton, David Maxwell Fyfe, Macmillan and Stanley the front bench representatives. Under Butler's brilliant chairmanship, they produced a document, *The Industrial Charter*, which was to be the basis of party policy for the next two decades. Its objective was 'to reconcile the need for central direction with the encouragement of individual effort' and gave respectability at last to many of the arguments Macmillan had voiced throughout the 1930s. One hostile critic described the document as 'a triumph for Mr Harold Macmillan. [He] once wrote a political treatise called *The Middle Way*. This is the second edition.' The party was undergoing national reform and reorganisation through the genius of Lord Woolton and the conference diehards were giving way to a younger, more radical element. By the late 1940s, Macmillan's views were at last orthodox expressions of party policy.

The relative freedom of Opposition gave him the opportunity to move beyond the confines of home politics. Since before the war he had held that Europe could survive only through cultural, economic and possibly political unity. When Churchill launched his non-party United Europe Movement in 1947, Macmillan joined its managing committee. The movement spread and gave birth in 1949 to the twelve-country Council of Europe on which Macmillan sat for three years as a Conservative delegate. He was deeply grieved by Labour's isolationist attitude, which kept Britain out of the Robert Schuman-inspired Coal and Steel Community when it was inaugurated, with six members, in April 1951. He was distressed, too, that many Conservatives were intransigently suspicious of any form of European integration. Eden was cool, and large sections of the party were convinced that any move in the direction of Europe would injure the Commonwealth.

It was ironic that Macmillan should play a highly effective role in overcoming resistance to Germany's participation, while powerless to persuade his own country to take up the challenge of providing imaginative leadership for European unity. He continued optimistic, encouraged by Britain's signature in 1949 of the North Atlantic Treaty, but could only hope that this military beginning would provide the base for economic and political alliance when Churchill, with his creative leadership, eventually came to power.

Yet the years of frustration in the European movement were not wasted. Macmillan renewed old friendships with wartime friends like Massigli and Monnet and, through conferences and visits to Germany, Italy and Scandinavia, he got to know 'almost every distinguished personality in Europe'. His cosmopolitan enthusiasm as well as his visionary approach to Western Europe earned him respect and augmented the reputation he had acquired in the Mediterranean in wartime. By the end of his period in Opposition his personal qualities had won him an international network of sympathetic contacts.

Nor did he limit himself to European affairs. In January 1947, in the twin capacities of publisher and politician, he visited Iran and India with John Wyndham. Macmillan's father had set up offices there in the 1880s and had many Indian friends, known to the son from their visits to England. Macmillan had supported Baldwin, not Churchill, on the 1935 India Act and he was sympathetic to the movement for self-determination.

In his weeks in India he visited six major cities and met – in addition to his publishing contacts – a wide range of senior Hindu and Moslem politicians (including Nehru and Jinnah) as well as British administrators. His conversations with this wide range of people reaffirmed his misgivings about the Labour Government's decision to give India independence as quickly as possible. He felt as he had felt about Greece: that one should not abandon one's responsibilities without making serious efforts first to guarantee a measure of stability. He was deeply pessimistic about the future when, on 20 February 1947, he learned that June 1948 had been fixed as the date for the British to pull out of India. He had been warned that a bloodbath would follow precipitate withdrawal, and the millions of Indian deaths that followed independence reinforced his conviction that post-war colonial problems required patient and delicate handling. The portents of change were clear in an era when Burma gained its independence, Ceylon became an independent dominion and Ireland left the Commonwealth. He had no desire to maintain the status quo, but he objected to the simple-minded view – shared by the left and the Americans alike – that took no account of racial, religious and tribal problems.

So although Macmillan supported many aspects of the Labour Government's foreign policy, on many issues he was a powerful critic. As their first term of Government came to an end, he found no difficulty in also condemning their conduct of economic affairs, for despite the benefits of Marshall Aid, Britain showed few signs of economic recovery from the disastrous impoverishment caused by war.

In the General Election of 1950 he fought again for a middle way that combined progress with freedom, and when the Labour majority over Conservatives fell to only eighteen, he felt confident that it could not last long. He harried the Government enthusiastically over the ensuing months. Attlee chose October 1951, and a Conservative victory was ensured when the campaign coincided with news of an unprecedented fall in Britain's gold and dollar reserves. Tired of

rationing that in some cases exceeded wartime levels, the voters responded to Churchill's slogan – 'Set the People Free' – and to a promise to increase house-building during the lifetime of the Government to 300,000 a year. The Tories were elected with an overall majority of seventeen.

Called to Chartwell, Macmillan found his Prime Minister in a tearful mood. 'He asked me to "build houses for the people".' Macmillan was taken aback: the job was recognised as a reckless and impossible manifesto commitment. Churchill grew emotional. As with the North Africa job, this was 'a great adventure'. '"It is a gamble – [it will] make or mar your political career. But every humble home will bless your name, if you succeed." More tears. I said I would think about it.'

His wife reminded him of his successes in the Ministry of Supply, and with re-awakening of the wartime spirit, Macmillan took up the challenge. Assured by his civil servants that 200,000 houses was the maximum annual target, he adopted the tactics of his old mentor, Lord Beaverbrook, falling back on improvisation, unorthodoxy and

*Above: Campaigning in the North. With the young Duke and Duchess of Northumberland by the walls of Alnwick Castle.*

*On the doorstep in Bromley before the 1951 General Election, one of our faithful supporters has agreed to display a poster.*

" ... 299,998 , 299,999 ... "

ruthlessness. 'The fault of most Ministers,' he said later, 'is not kicking over the traces; it is running too easily in the harness of Whitehall.' The mandarins had met their match.

In three happy years as Minister he dedicated himself totally to the achievement of the magic number. 'I could think – and even dream – of little else.' He chose his subordinates carefully. Ernest Marples – 'an exceptionally brilliant engineer and organiser' – was his Parliamentary Secretary. In the teeth of Civil Service opposition, he brought in for a year his old colleague, Sir Percy Mills – 'a first-class executive', bold and persistent. Looking at his department, he saw 'no urgency or drive; no production organisation, central or local; no progress officers; no machinery for identifying and breaking "bottlenecks"', and determined to put it virtually on a war footing.

Trade unions and management were brought into new Regional Housing Production Boards which revolutionised the building programme. Private builders were encouraged; repairs to dilapidated housing were undertaken; rent controls were eased to encourage landlords to modernise their property; new housing standards were simplified; cheaper designs were developed; productivity was increased; and when there proved to be insufficient capacity to produce bricks, he imported Italian labour. His officials stopped wringing their hands and joined in the excitement. Modest wagers were placed on the monthly housing figures.

In Cabinet he demanded the relaxation of restrictions that impeded him and, at a time of economic restraint, special treatment in the allocation of finance and raw materials. When his colleagues protested he sought and gained Churchill's support, threatening resignation when necessary. Knowing that his was the only measurable electoral pledge, the Cabinet gave in to him time and time again. At the party conference in October 1954 Macmillan announced that the target of 300,000 per year had been achieved – indeed exceeded – ahead of time. His reputation was made – in the party and nationally.

Not surprisingly, there were allegations that Macmillan had put career considerations before the national interest; but he was unmoved by such a charge. He cared passionately about providing decent homes for the less fortunate. In 1951 he used as a slogan a passage he had written in 1925: 'Housing is not a question of Conservatism or Socialism. It is a question of humanity.' From childhood, his guiding principle had been to do the job in hand to the best of his ability. This job had come from his Prime Minister, whose responsibility it was to determine priorities. His was to carry it out by any means available. Rising in the Tory Party pecking-order was no more than a marginal consideration.

*A post-war Housing Minister's dreams, as envisaged by Vicky.*

81

*The young Queen visiting an exhibition of modernised houses off Oxford Street in July 1954. Some of the 300,000 houses!*

*This sketch by Feliks Topolski was given to me in 1952 by my old friend and fellow 'European' Edward Beddington-Behrens.*

*1952. Inspecting the aftermath of the Lynmouth flood disaster. The Minister is expected to make a visit – to quite what effect I never really understood.*

He delighted in his success and was sincerely grateful to Churchill, 'who in peace as in war, had given me my chance'. But Churchill was losing his grip: in October 1954 he promoted Macmillan to a position of empty status – the Ministry of Defence.

A long-term defence programme had recently been agreed and Churchill, who had given him his head on housing, now looked over his shoulder. The power of the three Service Ministers effectively robbed Macmillan of other than co-ordinating functions, and the caretaker nature of the work was exacerbated by the general knowledge that Churchill's retirement, Eden's elevation and a reshuffle were imminent.

Macmillan's misery was compounded by those unpalatable aspects of Government policy which he had been able largely to ignore during his hectic days at Housing. Churchill had failed to give the hoped-for positive lead on Europe. Eden had steered the Cabinet's decision against joining the European Defence Community, and was planning further to reduce the feeble influence of the Council of Europe. Macmillan had contemplated resignation, but could not bring himself to be disloyal to Churchill in the old man's last days.

He had been aware for some time that Churchill was giving no leadership to his Cabinet, and had shown conspicuous courage in June by formally advising him to resign. He continued to tell him frankly that his early departure was vital to the future of the party. It was manifest that his advice was given in friendship, and no enmity resulted. Churchill resigned on 5 April 1955 and Macmillan gave up his office with relief after only six months. It had not been a wholly negative period. He had enjoyed renewing contacts with old military friends, and he had learned something of the nuclear arms debate. And although there had been little real work for him, Defence was a prestigious Ministry which enhanced his status in the party.

Eden acknowledged Macmillan's standing by making him Foreign Secretary. He was overjoyed at arriving at the 'summit of my ambition', despite Eden's frank admission that Salisbury would have been his choice had he not been a peer. Macmillan was confirmed in his job when the Conservatives won the May election (and to his father's delight, Maurice Macmillan won Halifax), and he expected to stay there throughout the Government's term. At last his international experience could be put to good use and he could make his mark as a constructive international statesman.

He soon found that, just as Churchill had liked to be his own Minister of Defence, so Eden liked to be his own Foreign Secretary. Eden was too courteous and their relationship too good for there to be any serious clash between them, but subordination meant a frustration which chafed.

*Before and after. In spite of appearances, the Minister did not personally carry out this particular kitchen improvement!*

In the short time he spent as Foreign Secretary, Macmillan's primary contribution was the setting up of a summit meeting in Geneva in July between America, Britain, France and the Soviet Union. He was convinced that the time was ripe for top-level formal meetings of this kind, and the weight he carried with Eisenhower and European leaders helped make this experiment possible. The idea of the summit – the first of its kind since the war – caused intense excitement and undue optimism in the international press. It failed to meet their expectations, but Macmillan was much struck by the generally amiable atmosphere in which the talks and informal contacts took place, and much cheered when the great nations accepted as an *assumpsit* that nuclear war could not be contemplated. That experience and subsequent international meetings confirmed him in certain views significant for the future. He became convinced of the importance of *détente* with Russia, and that progress towards disarmament depended on evolving a system of enforceable inspection and control. He also found himself perplexed by a new recognition: that since nuclear weapons preserved peace, disarmament might well make war more likely.

*Molotov signs the Vienna Treaty, 1955. John Forster Dulles is on the extreme left, and I am third from the right.*

Ambitions for his tenure of the Foreign Office were set aside in September, when Eden asked him to take over as Chancellor of the Exchequer from Butler, who had been under stress since the death of his wife.

On Lady Dorothy's advice, he persuaded Eden to postpone the reshuffle for a couple of months, and set out the terms on which he would accept the Exchequer. Mindful of his experiences at Defence and the Foreign Office, he demanded full support for his freedom of action as Chancellor, even though he did not propose to carry out his duties in an orthodox way: 'I must be, if not a revolutionary, something of a reformer.' (Though he added ruefully that 'to reform the Treasury is like trying to reform the Kremlin or the Vatican'.) He would not countenance the suggestion that Butler – now to be Lord Privy Seal and Leader of the House – should be Deputy Prime Minister. He regarded such a suggestion as unconstitutional and damaging to his own position as Chancellor: 'I must be undisputed head of the Home Front under you.' Eden – anxious at the same time to secure an effective Chancellor and a more pliable Foreign Secretary (in the person of Selwyn Lloyd) – agreed to all Macmillan's demands and on 22 December 1955 the reshuffle was announced. Macmillan made his attitude clear from the start. Brendan Bracken, who thought Macmillan 'a very remarkable man, imaginative, amusing and possessed of a judgement which is almost always wrong', spoke for the orthodox business community when he voiced his alarm at the prospect of squalls ahead. Less than three weeks after the Chancellor took office, Bracken told a friend, he had warned a number of newspaper moguls 'that in his judgement the bankers were a menace to the country' ... He also told them that he had crossed the floor of the House of Commons because of the deflationary policies of the bankers and Baldwin's Government and if this Government followed their bad example he would be perfectly prepared to cross the floor again.

Even allowing for exaggeration and misrepresentation, Macmillan was plainly making his stand early: he would not knuckle under to the City or the Treasury. It was a bad time for an expansionist to come into office. The economic state of the country was parlous and his first public act as Chancellor had perforce to be the announcement of a rise in the bank rate, the tightening of hire purchase restrictions and cuts in public expenditure and food subsidies. Once more, he had to fight for the measures inherent in doing the job correctly, for Eden opposed him on the food subsidies issue, and came to a compromise only because he was convinced Macmillan saw it as a resigning matter. Similarly with the Treasury: he immediately established an unprecedentedly close relationship with the Governor of the Bank of England and drew on informal outside advisers, including his old friend Mills and Sir Oliver Franks. When the Permanent Secretary retired, Macmillan insisted against all precedent on his being replaced by his old wartime subordinate, Sir Roger Makins, the British Ambassador in Washington.

He wanted his April budget to be revolutionary, but time was his enemy and in the event it proved largely uncontroversial except for the introduction of premium bonds. The theme of the budget was 'Savings' and Macmillan had demanded some new certificate or bond with an element of chance. Although it was condemned in some quarters as immoral or financially unsound, and by the Shadow Chancellor, Harold Wilson, as a 'squalid raffle', it proved to be a popular and lasting success.

During the summer Macmillan unsuccessfully pressed the case for wage restraint on the TUC. It was clear that his determination to be a wide-ranging and reforming Chancellor was undimmed by his initial experience of the restrictions of the job. In July, however, Nasser nationalised the Suez Canal Company, and Macmillan found a new preoccupation.

Through the ensuing months he was to be Eden's strongest supporter over the whole Suez adventure. While many of his colleagues who backed the use of force did so for financial reasons, Macmillan was haunted by the 1930s and saw Nasser as 'an Asiatic Mussolini'. He was a potent ally of the Prime Minister on the Cabinet Committee which dealt with Suez, and he reassured his colleagues that if armed intervention proved necessary, with American support there would be no flight from the pound.

Macmillan freely admits in his memoirs that he was wrong in his assessment of the American reaction to Suez. In the post-war years he had had only occasional contact with Eisenhower, and though he had a good and improving relationship with John Foster Dulles, he underestimated American disapproval of any British action that smacked of the old colonialism.

He used his old contacts to promote Eden's policy. When Robert Murphy came to London to investigate the Suez question, Macmillan assured him that force would be used if necessary. His object was to frighten the United States, convincing them of the gravity with which Britain viewed Nasser's action. That achieved, Macmillan felt, the Americans would rally to the British cause. In America for a meeting with the International Monetary Fund (IMF) in September, Macmillan saw both Eisenhower and Dulles and stressed that Britain would at all costs carry the dispute through to a successful conclusion. Again he underestimated the force of their opposition. He was too inexperienced in modern American politics to realise that the forthcoming American election was their main preoccupation, and that Eisenhower's cordiality reflected their old friendship rather than signalling support when it counted.

When the French came up with the proposal to collude secretly with an Israeli attack on Egypt, thus giving the British and French an excuse to intervene – separating the combatants and hence securing control of the Canal – Macmillan was strongly in favour. On 29 October Israel attacked Sinai and two days later Britain bombed the Egyptian airforce virtually out of existence. The Anglo-French invasion commenced a few days later. Although their military capacity was not in doubt, on 6 November the Cabinet ordered a ceasefire and agreed to hand over to the United Nations.

The ostensible reason for this *volte-face* was that Israel and Egypt had ceased fighting. In fact Britain had no option but to call off her action, for she had suffered a crippling run on the pound. Help from the United States or the IMF was made conditional upon withdrawal. Macmillan was as strongly in favour of pulling out as he had been of going in. The change in his attitudes shocked many onlookers on both sides. Bracken wrote to Beaverbrook on 22 November that Macmillan's original bellicosity 'had been beyond description . . . today he might be described as the leader of the bolters'. As Macmillan recalls the period in his memoirs, ' "First in, first out" was to be the elegant expression of one of my chief Labour critics on many subsequent occasions.'

The whole episode reflects two strains in Macmillan's character – the romantic and the pragmatic. Retrospectively defending the Government's action in the House on 12 November 1956, he argued against drift when a decision had to be taken: 'Then it is the brave man chooses, while the coward turns aside.' Yet he believed in courage, not foolhardiness. Once it was clear that he had misread the position, and that only bankruptcy could result from a pursuance of the adventure, he pushed for a swift and decisive withdrawal. His position can best be summed up by a remark he once made on a wholly different issue: 'It is only to petty minds that consistency is a necessary or even desirable attribute to statesmanship.'

# The Emergence of 'Supermac'

On 8 January 1957 ill health forced Eden to resign. The bond between Macmillan and Eden was strong: they had both suffered in the First War and had been united in the late 1930s in their opposition to appeasement. Macmillan admired Eden's courage and integrity and thought it a personal tragedy that the Prime Ministership for which he had waited so long should end so soon in failure. But it was clear to all the Cabinet that Eden's showing over Suez made his resignation inevitable.

It was a twist of political fate that Macmillan's support for the Suez adventure, which had split the party and the country, should be the cause of his succeeding Eden. Rab Butler had been acting Prime Minister while Eden was in Jamaica trying to recover his strength. His experience and national prestige caused almost all the press to tip him as successor. Yet Macmillan's robust defence of the Government's actions had proved far more popular with the Tory Party than had Butler's equivocation.

After the Cabinet meeting on 9 January at which Eden announced his resignation, Salisbury (Lord President) and Lord Kilmuir (Lord Chancellor) assumed responsibility for assessing party opinion. Every member of the Cabinet other than the two contenders was called before them and asked by Salisbury, 'Well, which is it to be, Wab or Hawold?' The majority opted for 'Hawold', as did those consulted on back-bench and constituency opinion. So, too, did Eden and Churchill, whom the Queen consulted personally. Macmillan's courage and decisiveness appear to have been the factors that generally weighed most heavily.

Unaware of the progress of the canvass, Macmillan spent the morning of 10 January at home in No. 11, calming his nerves by re-reading *Pride and Prejudice*. At midday a call came from Buckingham Palace requesting him to wait upon the Queen at 2.00. In accepting the appointment he warned her that he could not guarantee to be in office for longer than six weeks. 'As I drove back to No. 11, I thought chiefly of my poor mother.'

*Returning from the great Commonwealth tour in February 1958 to a warm welcome from the crowds at No. 10.*

93

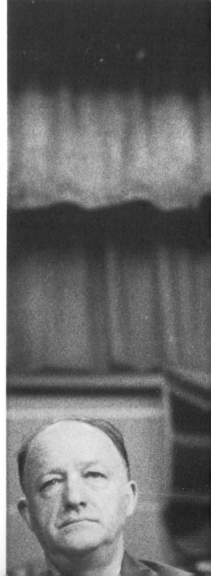

Left: *While I have never been keen on sport for sport's sake, relaxation in the open air provided a welcome change from London. Here I am during the first summer break as Prime Minister, grouse shooting with Rab at Philip Swinton's in Yorkshire.*

He immediately set about the business of choosing a Cabinet, a job requiring a great deal of hard thought and a few painful decisions. He had an early taste of the image the press was to purvey of him: he took his Chief Whip, Edward Heath, to the Turf Club for a dinner of game pie and champagne, an event widely publicised as evidence of the reactionary régime now in command. Yet several of his appointments were daring and imaginative. Percy Mills was given a peerage and brought in as Minister of Power. Ernest Marples was made Postmaster General. Edward Boyle, who had resigned over Suez, was persuaded to take a Parliamentary Secretaryship at Education, for 'I never felt that sincere disaffection should be held against a young Member.' The three Service Ministers appointed were told their jobs had been reduced in status, and Duncan Sandys was made Minister of Defence with instructions to undertake a drastic overhaul of his responsibilities. The leader of the Tory left-wing, Butler, was appointed to the sensitive Home Office. And, to make room for younger men, Macmillan despatched his brother-in-law Stuart and one of his oldest friends, Gwilym Lloyd George, to the Lords.

It always amused Macmillan that memories were so short, and people so influenced by trivial reporting of his affluence and Edwardian style, that he was seen as a bastion of the right. Moreover, he found it a useful smoke-screen for his unchanged radicalism, permitting actions and utterances that would otherwise have had the right baying for his blood. When on 22 January he made a speech to some thousand of the party faithful after his formal election to the leadership, there was no nervous reaction to words that should have left any detached listener in no doubt about where his loyalties lay. After praising the party for its tolerance of differing views, he went on to express its fundamental philosophy. 'To use Disraeli's phrase, we must be conservative to conserve all that is good and radical to uproot all that is bad. So it is that we have never been, and I trust that while I am your leader we never will be a party of any class or sectional

*After Suez, the Party needed lifting, but Rab doesn't look convinced. Llandudno Conference, 1956.*

interest.' The hallmark of the Conservatives was that 'We believe that unless we give opportunity to the strong and able we shall never have the means to provide real protection for the weak and old.'

If his followers on the right found comfort in his upper-class and old-fashioned manner, those on the left were to be somewhat consoled for the defeat of Butler by the substance rather than the veneer of his Prime Ministership. The Labour Party never saw through him. They took him at face value, as an easy-going anachronism with an amateur's approach to the serious business of Government. Harold Wilson made generous amends when he admitted in a review of Macmillan's last volume of memoirs that 'Those of us were wrong who regarded him as a *"Premier Ministre fainéant"*. He was utterly hard-working.'

Those who worked with him in No. 10 were in no doubt about that. His Private Secretaries knew that he rarely took more than a day or two away from his grinding schedule and that, whatever the length of his working day, the contents of the red boxes were read and mastered, crucial decisions taken, and succinct instructions given late at night or early in the morning. He never got immersed in detail and he was a superb delegator, but he saved time only to have more for reflecting on long-term problems and instigating moves towards their solution. 'Quiet, calm deliberation disentangles every knot' was the motto he wrote out and pinned to the door between the Cabinet room and that of the Private Secretaries. It was an approach which as a nervous man he had adopted consciously and it had served him well. He loathed fuss and, when he had taken a particularly difficult decision, he would withdraw with a favourite book and thus make himself ready for the next challenge. Self-knowledge was one of Macmillan's greatest strengths: he knew precisely how to recharge his batteries. In the Mediterranean he had retired for at least one day a month to sleep and read. Then, as now, he was untroubled if reading during working hours was seen as frivolous and irresponsible.

The change from subordinate to leader was congenial in every way but one. He found himself rather solitary, 'for very few people ask to see a Prime Minister except those he does not much want to see'. He had no leisure to drop in frequently at his clubs, and his office in any case was an inhibiting factor in maintaining informal relationships. The nearest he could get to the old life was lunch twice a week at the Carlton, at what was known as the 'Parliamentary Table', where he could suspend discretion to gossip with people he trusted. Otherwise, he relied for informal discussions mainly on his No. 10 staff, in whom he came to have total confidence. He talked freely also to Churchill – as much for his valued guidance as for the love he bore the old man, who, he knew, needed to be kept in touch.

*An infrequent but stylish performer at the crease – even wearing shooting shoes – at a charity match to raise money for the McIndoe Burns Unit at East Grinstead.*

*Unfortunately I never really had time to play a lot of golf, but Dorothy and I played together in Scotland. I suspect that this drive at the ninth on the King's Course at Gleneagles may have gone astray. We were staying with Billy Rootes in Perthshire in 1958.*

Below: *We got away in April 1964 after I came out of hospital and managed some fishing. The salmon was not caught on a fly, I fear.*

His other great support was his family. His wife was not only indefatigable and an excellent judge of people, but also brought an informality to No. 10 that Macmillan much appreciated. In the Devonshire tradition she loved the company of children, and their eleven grandchildren (the progeny of Maurice and Kate Macmillan, Carol and Julian Faber and Catherine and Julian Amery) were frequent visitors there, tricycles and scooters in the front hall forming a constant hazard. Macmillan had to warn some of his grandsons not to obstruct the arrival of Ambassadors or Cabinet Ministers while playing draughts with the policemen. He enjoyed having the children around, and had time to get to know some of them better than he had his own children.

Left: *Christmas 1957. What a pleasure to get home after nearly a year at No. 10. But even then the demands of the press were insatiable. We all look very uncomfortable and only the babies are natural.*

*On the stairs: Alexander Macmillan; Louise Amery; Dorothy with Leo Amery on her knee and Teresa Amery sitting by her; Anne Faber with Lizzie Amery.*

*Standing left to right: Mark Faber; Adam Macmillan; Joshua Macmillan and Michael Faber; and on the floor, David Macmillan.*

Right: *Dorothy and myself in the drawing room at No. 10 before it had to be rebuilt owing to the decay of the foundations.*

Previous page, above: *With some of the grandchildren in the garden at Birch Grove in the summer of 1956.*

*From left to right: Joshua Macmillan; Adam Macmillan; self; Anne Faber with Teresa Amery on her knee; Alexander Macmillan; Dorothy with Rachel Macmillan; and Michael Faber. Sitting right at the front are Louise Amery and Mark Faber.*

During his first few weeks of office Macmillan recognised that the most pressing priorities were to restore public confidence in the Government, to clear up the political mess left by Suez and find an accord with Egypt that would enable British ships to use the canal again, and to restore the old spirit of co-operation with the United States. Of these, the third was the most urgent. Macmillan felt that without American support he would be hamstrung in the exercise of foreign policy and unable to give the country any firm indication that he was in control. He understood why Americans thought Britain had behaved recklessly and wrongly over Suez but, like many of his countrymen, he felt badly let down by the vacillation and self-righteousness they had displayed. He had responded warmly to Eisenhower's friendly congratulations on his appointment, and was searching for an opportunity to exploit their old comradeship. Yet he was determined not to don a white sheet and appear in the guise of a supplicant. He waited for Eisenhower to make overtures, and they came soon and generously. On 22 January Eisenhower suggested a meeting in Washington or Bermuda between 21 and 24 March, to discuss 'all the great issues confronting the world'. Relieved and grateful, Macmillan opted for the British territory of Bermuda.

The Foreign Secretary, Selwyn Lloyd, accompanied him and joined in the talks with Eisenhower and Dulles, but Macmillan had many private chats with the President, during which their old friendship was revived and strengthened. He found Eisenhower a lonely figure, delighted to have someone to talk to freely. The specific gains from Bermuda were US agreements to join the Military Committee of the Baghdad Pact between Britain, Iraq, Iran, Pakistan and Turkey, and to supply Britain with guided missiles while approving her continuance of nuclear tests. More important, Britain and America would henceforward co-ordinate their policies in the United Nations, and Eisenhower and Macmillan would write privately and regularly to each other on international issues that worried them.

This *rapprochement* was of crucial importance to Macmillan's performance as Prime Minister. He took every opportunity to build on it, and was able to take all his decisions on foreign policy knowing precisely where America stood. During the summer, when, in response to an appeal from the Sultan of Oman, Britain sent help to put down a rebellion, and when Dulles threatened to intervene militarily in the Levant to deal with Communist infiltration, the allies kept each other informed of their intentions every step of the way.

The confidence that Macmillan gained from Bermuda was tested by a potential crisis immediately after his return. He and his Colonial Secretary, Alan Lennox-Boyd, had decided to release Archbishop Makarios from detention in the Seychelles in the hope of damping

*In Bermuda Ike and I were to talk about 'all the great issues confronting the world', but I don't think we touched on cabbages or kings.*

'THE TIME HAS COME', THE WALRUS SAID, 'TO TALK OF MANY THINGS :'
— FROM LEWIS CARROLL'S THROUGH THE LOOKING GLASS

Below: *In Washington in March 1959, Ike took Selwyn and me to see Foster (Dulles) in the Walter Reed Hospital, where he had recently had an operation. The photographers found a 'suitable' setting for this slightly artificial conversation piece.*

*In June 1958 I visited President Eisenhower in Washington* (left) *to discuss detente. In November he sent his young and ambitious Vice-President, Richard Nixon, to London* (above) *when he presented me with this picture taken at the earlier meeting.*

Overleaf: *A somewhat low-key protest in Wolverhampton, March 1958. Within five years we had obliged the lady and the Nuclear Test Ban Treaty had been signed.*

down Greek terrorism in Cyprus. Macmillan's reading of history – particularly that of Ireland – had convinced him 'that coercion alone could not be the answer', and he was prepared to make a conciliatory gesture in the hope of bringing a future settlement nearer. His Lord President, Salisbury, viewed the gesture as weakness and came to Macmillan to protest 'in one of his resigning moods'. Macmillan, although he regretted the loss of his old friend, showed who was boss by promptly accepting his resignation.

On 1 April he had to report on Bermuda to the Commons. It was a debate to which the Opposition were looking forward, for in addition to the resignation of one of their most senior statesmen, the Conservatives were suffering from a series of poor performances in by-elections and the outbreak of ship-building and engineering strikes, while Nasser had announced terms for reopening the canal that put Britain in an embarrassing position. Macmillan was even more nervous than usual, for to fail in the debate would be to forfeit the good opinion of Tory MPs, vital to the process of restoring the party's confidence nationwide. In the event he succeeded magnificently. By astutely focusing attention on the issue of nuclear tests,

106

he showed up divisions within the Labour Party on nuclear weapons, and united the Tories in delighted appreciation of their opponents' discomfiture. It was a tactic he employed again on 16 May, at another time of vulnerability. Having accepted Nasser's terms and instructed British ships not to boycott the canal, he was under attack from a small group of right-wingers including Salisbury. Once again he found a pretext to divide the Opposition on nuclear tests. From then on, his mastery of the House was an accepted fact. In speeches and answers to parliamentary questions he dominated by a combination of thorough preparation, quick-wittedness and a knowledge of his opponents' weak points built up over many years of constant observation.

He celebrated by asking Wyndham to come and work for him again. He had been without him at the Treasury, for Wyndham was pursuing a private dispute over death duties and had therefore had to retire. Now he explained that he had not asked him before 'to rejoin the old firm' because he 'did not really think my administration could last more than a few weeks; but we seem now to have got over quite a number of jumps in this Grand National course, and having just managed to pull the old mare through the brook and somehow got to the other side with the same jockey up, and the Cecil colours fallen, I am plucking up my courage.' Wyndham accepted with alacrity, to work immensely hard for – at his request – no remuneration.

Even before he felt secure, Macmillan had been prepared to take risks. Sandys's Defence White Paper, published in April, had been as drastic as requested. It included plans to cut expenditure heavily on conventional forces (including the abolition of National Service in 1960) and to rely much more heavily on nuclear weapons. It was a strategy of which Macmillan fully approved, for he believed that unmatchable Soviet superiority in conventional forces left nuclear deterrence as the only protection in Europe. This view was lent credibility by the enthusiasm with which the Russians were advocating international nuclear disarmament, and particularly an immediate ban on nuclear tests, a series of which they had completed, while the British had only just started. Macmillan was not opposed to the basic principle behind the ban, for he was concerned about pollution from atmospheric tests, but he had no wish to expedite the matter until parity was restored.

There were many issues in 1958 on which he sought thus to hold the line rather than launch initiatives. The Treaty of Rome had been signed in March, and the Common Market was due to come into force on 1 January 1958. Macmillan never ceased to regret Britain's self-imposed exclusion from the Six (which had emerged from the

*The Old Fox comes to London. Welcoming Konrad Adenauer, the Federal German Chancellor, in April 1958 when he was eighty-two.*

*To Paris in June 1958 for the infamous U2 Summit. In response to Khrushchev's protests about the American spy-plane, General de Gaulle accused the Soviet sputnik of violating 'the sacred airspace of France' in its earth orbit.*

beginnings in coal and steel), and his conception of European unity was that it should embrace the maximum number of members – a state of affairs made unlikely by the terms of the treaty. His Chancellor of the Exchequer, Peter Thorneycroft, had worked out at the Board of Trade under Eden plans for a system of European free trade that led in 1959 to the creation of the European Free Trade Area (EFTA). Macmillan appointed Reginald Maudling in August 1957 as a Cabinet Minister responsible for Britain's interest in Europe. His brief was to evolve some formula of association between the Six and the proposed EFTA, although Macmillan did not want to push the matter until he got to know the European leaders better and saw how the Treaty of Rome would work out in practice. French Government instability, before de Gaulle took power in June 1958, made Maudling's task harder, and no real progress on the issue was made until Macmillan's second term as Prime Minister.

After several visits to Europe, Macmillan was happy by the end of 1958 that he had a good personal understanding with Adenauer and, despite the speed at which French Governments changed, Anglo-French co-operation was much improved. He had managed to alleviate some of the European suspicion about Britain's relationship

*The look of amusement on Dorothy's face is understandable. I never took part in even al fresco cuisine at home. I hope that young Greg Clapham appreciated the honour. The cook-out took place at Banyak Suka in Queensland, Australia, in February 1958.*

with the United States and her role in the Commonwealth. Meanwhile he had succeeded at the Commonwealth Prime Ministers' Conference in London in mid-summer in reassuring individual members about the implications of any putative formal arrangements in Europe. The conference had also brought home to him how rapidly the Commonwealth was changing and how little he knew about it. True to form, he decided to find out for himself by undertaking a Commonwealth tour for five weeks from January 1958. His purpose he summarised in these words as being 'to listen, to see and to learn; to meet many old friends and to make many new ones; and in a series of informal talks, as well as by public appearances, help co-operation and understanding between the countries of the Commonwealth'.

No Prime Minister had ever undertaken such a tour, and a weaker man would have cancelled it on the eve of departure. During 1957 his Government had had some problems on the economic front. A run on the pound early on had led to an increase of 2% in the bank rate, cuts in public expenditure and a credit squeeze. In December 1957 the Chancellor demanded cuts of £153 million in public expenditure and refused to accept the Cabinet's proffered compromise of £100 million. Macmillan felt he was exhibiting 'fanatical rigidity', and himself stood firm. On 6 January, Thorneycroft, his Economic Secretary Nigel Birch, and his Financial Secretary Enoch Powell, all tendered their resignations. Macmillan appointed the Minister of Agriculture, Derick Heathcoat Amory, as Thorneycroft's successor, and set off the following day for India. At the airport he explained to the reporters who had gathered there: 'the best thing to do was to settle up these little local difficulties and then to turn to the wider vision of the Commonwealth.' The phrase 'little local difficulties' hit the headlines and brought the 'unflappable' image to national attention.

In five weeks, Macmillan and Lady Dorothy covered 33,000 miles and visited India, Pakistan, Ceylon, Singapore, New Zealand and Australia. Physically and mentally exhausting as it was, the trip proved to be exhilarating. Both the Macmillans discovered an unexpected capacity within themselves to enjoy the greetings of large crowds and to respond effectively and simply to gestures of goodwill from people of every nationality. It was a royal progress rather than a political tour. The fact that such a considerable amount of time and effort were being expended by a British Prime Minister was deeply appreciated in all the countries that he and Lady Dorothy visited, and Macmillan himself derived great benefit from the wide-ranging conversations he was able to have with Commonwealth leaders and senior officials.

*India, January 1958.* Right:
*With Mr Jawaharlal Nehru,
driving through the noble Lutyens
Government buildings in New
Delhi.* Below: *Being garlanded is
a flattering but somewhat
uncomfortable experience, as the
garlands are very wet to keep them
fresh, and frequently contain
residents who rapidly avail
themselves of the opportunity to
crawl out. As soon as I was out of
sight of these children at Delhi
Airport, I removed the garlands
and, I hope, any visitors.*

FRONTIER OF PAKISTAN
TRAVELLERS ARE NOT PERMITTED TO PASS
THIS NOTICE BOARD
UNLESS THEY HAVE COMPLIED WITH
THE PASSPORT REGULATIONS

Above: *The gates to the Khyber Pass. Despite appearances, I was not leading an invasion of Pakistan from Afghanistan.*

*Receiving a home-made rifle, based on the Lee-Enfield, which had been forged over an open fire by the Maliks of the North-West frontier. As many a British soldier in the past and many a Soviet soldier today can testify, they shoot just as straight as the factory product – probably straighter.*

113

114

*A display by the Pakistan Air Force underlined the potential for hostility between her and India. The Commonwealth has its share of tensions and divisions like any family, I fear.*

Australia was another port of call on our 1958 Commonwealth tour. Left: *Clearly an important local personage, who could prove useful politically when one finds oneself in deep water.*

Below: *Australian journalists are as adept at bowling a fast one as their cricketers, but handling them is clearly a matter of judicious umpiring!*

*Speaking at the State dinner in Melbourne. Bob Menzies appreciates the story, but I fear Dorothy has heard it before.*

*We did not in fact take home one for each of the grandchildren!*

117

*I say goodbye to Ghana at the end of my visit.*

When he returned he felt that the future of the Commonwealth must depend on personal as well as formal relations; Governor-Generals and High Commissioners must be selected for ability; the transformation from the old colonial Empire to a new Commonwealth must be brought about peaceably 'in faith and hope'; and Britain had a duty to interpret the new members to the old. Most important of all, he believed that the vision of numerous races and creeds working together in co-operation might be made to appeal to contemporary youth.

It was apparent to onlookers that Macmillan had grown in confidence and stature. Following on his success with Eisenhower and Adenauer in particular, he now felt secure and well informed enough to play some part in world affairs as an initiator rather than a reactor. He appreciated the pitfalls, and it was a feature of his diplomacy that European, American and Commonwealth allies remained fully informed of his thinking and his plans. He took no action without the widest possible consultation, and responded enthusiastically to any invitation, of a public or private nature, to meet political leaders face to face.

It was not roses all the way. On many issues progress with the United States was halting. It was impossible to agree on the Middle East; crises were simply dealt with as they arose. Yet the Eisenhower–Macmillan understanding carried them through. Britain backed America's action in sending the 6th Fleet to Beirut in July to help the Lebanese President restore stability. America backed Britain's decision to send paratroopers to the assistance of King Hussein of Jordan – 'a quixotic but honourable undertaking'.

There was a fundamental difference, too, over Asia. America refused to trade with Communist China, which Britain had recognised in 1950. When the mainland Government began in August 1958 to bombard the off-shore island of Quemoy, Chiang Kai-Shek's territory, the Americans were bellicose. Macmillan feared a dangerous military confrontation, but he gave the Americans moral support which helped Dulles to perform brilliantly in brinkmanship and, in the spring of 1959, the bombardment ceased.

*Welcoming King Hussein to 10 Downing Street in April 1959, the first time that I met the Jordanian monarch whom I was to visit in Amman in 1983.*

*How happy could I be with either,*
*Were t'other dear charmer away!*

Private encouragement from Eisenhower and various Common-wealth and European leaders bolstered Macmillan in his progress towards a breaking of the Cyprus deadlock. In autumn 1957 he had offered the Governorship to Sir Hugh Foot, whose political radical-ism he hoped 'might assist rather than retard the search for some solution'. Finding a system of partition that would be acceptable to both Greeks and Turks and also allow for the maintenance in Cyprus of British military bases took over two years of often disheartening negotiations. Macmillan's visit to Athens, Ankara and Cyprus in August 1958 was apparently fruitless. Yet in 1960, Cyprus became an independent republic under a Greek Cypriot President – Makarios – and a Turkish Cypriot vice-president – Kütchük. It was a compromise that owed a great deal to his instinct for when to stand firm and when to give ground gracefully.

Left: *Macheath's quandary in*
The Beggar's Opera *symbolised
the problem of pleasing both
Greece and Turkey over the
partition of Cyprus.*

121

Perhaps his greatest practical triumph during his first period of office as Prime Minister was the repeal in July 1958 of the 1946 McMahon Act in America which had hindered the US in passing on atomic information to the British. Now the way was clear to the development of a common nuclear programme – a development Macmillan had long wanted as a defence against Russian aggression. He was concerned nonetheless that it should be complemented by progress towards *détente*. On taking office he had refused to carry out a planned Prime Ministerial visit to Russia, but he now felt that he should soon make such a gesture.

Had he not been on excellent terms with American and European leaders, the visit would have been impossible: Khrushchev had achieved supreme power in March 1958 and was flexing his muscles over Berlin. Yet Macmillan knew his allies shared his worries about the deterioration in relations with Moscow and they put no serious obstacles in his way. He had earned sufficient trust to be regarded as a reliable mediator. When a formal invitation was sought and extended in January 1959, Macmillan had the added pleasure of having caused a degree of left-wing chagrin at home. He was himself a little

*My Russian visit, February 1959. Above: Under the fixed, but not I think malevolent gaze of the Red Army, with the great survivor Anastas Mikoyan on my arrival in Leningrad. Right: 'No, after you.' Meeting Khrushchev in Moscow. The hat, worn in 1940 when supporting the Finns against the Soviets, struck a certain ironic note.*

fearful lest some unexpected disaster result from this initiative, but he felt that at the very least it would be 'a great adventure; it might also be great fun'.

He arrived on 21 February on what was described as a 'voyage of discovery', and spent eleven gruelling days during which Khrushchev alternated between expressions of warm friendship, calculated insults and attempts to divide him from his allies. There were moments of high farce, including an episode when Macmillan was crammed with his host into a round wicker basket to coast down an ice mound. He found Khrushchev 'a kind of mixture between Peter the Great and Lord Beaverbrook' – 'an excitable, petulant, occasionally impossible, but not unlovable extrovert'. Macmillan ignored insults that would have caused a man more worried about his own dignity to storm home in high dudgeon. At the end of the trip a joint *communiqué* acknowledged that there was no agreement on Berlin, but that Russia had agreed to Macmillan's suggestion: a meeting of Russian and Western Foreign Ministers to draw up plans for a Summit Conference to discuss a nuclear test ban.

124

On his return, Macmillan flew to Paris, Bonn, Washington and Ottawa to report on his trip. The meeting of the Foreign Ministers was agreed for May, and though it made little progress it was followed up by an agreement between Eisenhower and Khrushchev to exchange personal visits with a view to narrowing the difference between them. Khrushchev's visit to Washington in September brought about a reduction in tension over Berlin and a Summit was agreed for 16 May 1960. Eisenhower and Macmillan were optimistic; Adenauer and de Gaulle pessimistic. But Macmillan felt that his time had not been wasted: there was a perceptible thaw in East–West relations.

As an international statesman, he was doing a job that could be done by no one else. In home affairs, while he took responsibility for a strategic leadership, he was content to delegate a great deal, but he was eternally aware that he had to call an election by the spring of 1960. Under his chairmanship, a steering committee of senior Ministers had, since 1957, handled political strategy, and a subgroup including Maudling and Powell had more recently developed detailed policies for inclusion in the manifesto. Remembering what Woolton had done for the party's fortunes ten years earlier, Macmillan had appointed the extrovert, inspiring Hailsham as Chairman in mid-1957 and the constituency organisation had responded enthusiastically.

Left: *My war-time colleague Eisenhower visited me at Chequers in August 1959, and we drove in what seems reckless insecurity down Fleet Street.*

*The Prime Minister ignores his constituents at his peril. At a Conservative Party fête in Bromley in June 1957, trying my luck at the hoop-la stall. The rather exotic young ladies flanking me were Miss Diane Lancaster, Queen of the Fête, and her attendants.*

On the economic front there had been a gradual improvement in 1958 permitting a reduction in the bank rate and the removal of credit controls. Heathcoat Amory had proved to be a Chancellor after Macmillan's own expansionist heart, and had presented in the spring the most generous peacetime budget ever. Macmillan was aware of the political benefits, always having the view that a flat budget before an election was weak and defeatist. An election was the time to take imaginative risks. Yet there was nothing cynical in the pressure he put on Amory to make the budget more attractive. Mamillan was still regretful that he had not ignored the Treasury and expanded the economy earlier.

He announced a General Election for 8 October 1959 at a time when the country had virtually full employment, a strong balance of payments and stable prices that owed a great deal to the firm resistance the Minister of Labour, Iain Macleod, had put up to inflationary wage demands. The message of the Conservative manifesto was summarised thus: 'Do you want to go ahead on the lines which have brought you prosperity at home? Do you want your present leaders to represent you abroad?'

*Karsh's portrait, a personal favourite of mine.*

126

Left: *At a constituency fête in Bromley, a ride on a miniature train, with the inevitable jokes about 'Don't go off the rails' - very appropriate for a former director of the Great Western.*

Above: *It was a relief to get away from Whitehall to real people with real concerns.*

Right: *At Admiralty House during the rebuilding of No. 10. The boxes that tie a Minister to his office wherever he goes.*

Below: *The Amery twins, Leo and Lizzie, with their sister Teresa, Birch Grove, April 1961.*

Above: *A. R. Thomson's painting* The Debate on the Address, 1st November 1960.

Left: *The Commonwealth Prime Ministers' Conference, 26 June 1957. Standing: De Silva (Minister of Justice, Ceylon), Macdonald (Minister of External Affairs, New Zealand), Louw (Minister of External Affairs, South Africa), Welensky (Rhodesia). Seated: Nkrumah (Ghana), Nehru (India), Diefenbaker (Canada), self, Menzies (Australia), Suhrawardy (Pakistan). I found little difficulty in establishing a genuine sense of harmony even among many views, some of which were naturally divergent.*

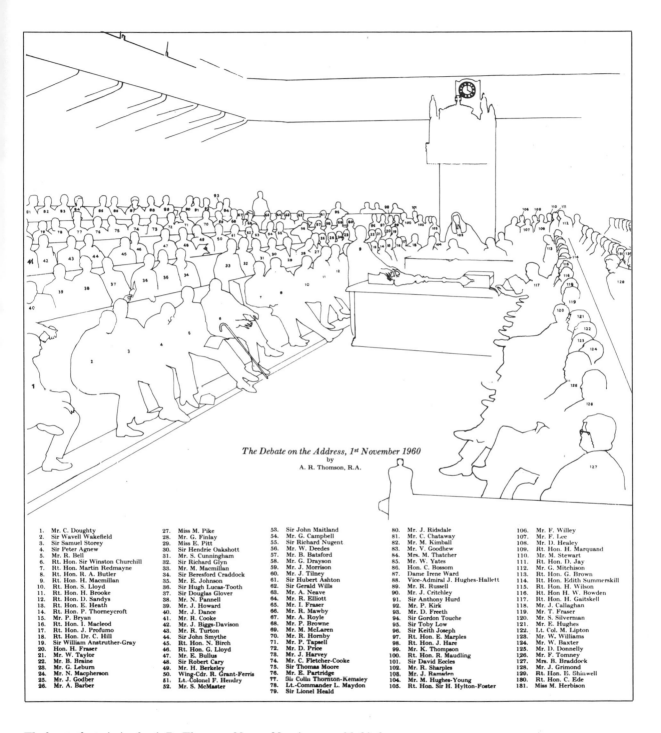

*The Debate on the Address, 1st November 1960*
by
A. R. Thomson, R.A.

| | | | | |
|---|---|---|---|---|
| 1. Mr. C. Doughty | 27. Miss M. Pike | 53. Sir John Maitland | 80. Mr. J. Ridsdale | 106. Mr. F. Willey |
| 2. Sir Wavell Wakefield | 28. Mr. G. Finlay | 54. Mr. G. Campbell | 81. Mr. C. Chataway | 107. Mr. F. Lee |
| 3. Sir Samuel Storey | 29. Miss E. Pitt | 55. Sir Richard Nugent | 82. Mr. M. Kimball | 108. Mr. D. Healey |
| 4. Sir Peter Agnew | 30. Sir Hendrie Oakshott | 56. Mr. W. Deedes | 83. Mr. V. Goodhew | 109. Rt. Hon. H. Marquand |
| 5. Mr. R. Bell | 31. Mr. S. Cunningham | 57. Mr. B. Batsford | 84. Mrs. M. Thatcher | 110. Mr. M. Stewart |
| 6. Rt. Hon. Sir Winston Churchill | 32. Sir Richard Glyn | 58. Mr. G. Drayson | 85. Mr. W. Yates | 111. Rt. Hon. D. Jay |
| 7. Rt. Hon. Martin Redmayne | 33. Mr. M. Macmillan | 59. Mr. J. Morrison | 86. Hon. C. Bossom | 112. Mr. G. Mitchison |
| 8. Rt. Hon. R. A. Butler | 34. Sir Beresford Craddock | 60. Mr. J. Tilney | 87. Dame Irene Ward | 113. Rt. Hon. G. Brown |
| 9. Rt. Hon. H. Macmillan | 35. Mr. E. Johnson | 61. Sir Hubert Ashton | 88. Vice-Admiral J. Hughes-Hallett | 114. Rt. Hon. Edith Summerskill |
| 10. Rt. Hon. S. Lloyd | 36. Sir Hugh Lucas-Tooth | 62. Sir Gerald Wills | 89. Mr. R. Russell | 115. Rt. Hon. H. Wilson |
| 11. Rt. Hon. H. Brooke | 37. Mr. A. Neave | 63. Mr. A. Neave | 90. Mr. J. Critchley | 116. Rt. Hon H. W. Bowden |
| 12. Rt. Hon. D. Sandys | 38. Mr. N. Pannell | 64. Mr. R. Elliott | 91. Sir Anthony Hurd | 117. Rt. Hon. H. Gaitskell |
| 13. Rt. Hon. E. Heath | 39. Mr. I. Fraser | 65. Mr. I. Fraser | 92. Mr. P. Kirk | 118. Mr. J. Callaghan |
| 14. Rt. Hon. P. Thorneycroft | 40. Mr. J. Dance | 66. Mr. R. Mawby | 93. Mr. D. Freeth | 119. Mr. T. Fraser |
| 15. Mr. P. Bryan | 41. Mr. R. Cooke | 67. Mr. A. Royle | 94. Sir Gordon Touche | 120. Mr. S. Silverman |
| 16. Rt. Hon. I. Macleod | 42. Mr. J. Biggs-Davison | 68. Mr. P. Browne | 95. Sir Toby Low | 121. Mr. E. Hughes |
| 17. Rt. Hon. J. Profumo | 43. Mr. R. Turton | 69. Mr. M. McLaren | 96. Sir Keith Joseph | 122. Lt.-Col. M. Lipton |
| 18. Rt. Hon. Dr. C. Hill | 44. Sir John Smythe | 70. Mr. R. Hornby | 97. Rt. Hon. E. Marples | 123. Mr. W. Williams |
| 19. Sir William Anstruther-Gray | 45. Rt. Hon. N. Birch | 71. Mr. P. Tapsell | 98. Rt. Hon. J. Hare | 124. Mr. W. Baxter |
| 20. Hon. H. Fraser | 46. Rt. Hon. G. Lloyd | 72. Mr. D. Price | 99. Mr. K. Thompson | 125. Mr. D. Donnelly |
| 21. Mr. W. Taylor | 47. Mr. E. Bullus | 73. Mr. J. Harvey | 100. Rt. Hon. R. Maudling | 126. Mr. F. Tomney |
| 22. Mr. B. Braine | 48. Sir Robert Cary | 74. Mr. C. Fletcher-Cooke | 101. Sir David Eccles | 127. Mrs. B. Braddock |
| 23. Mr. G. Leburn | 49. Mr. H. Berkeley | 75. Sir Thomas Moore | 102. Mr. R. Sharples | 128. Mr. J. Grimond |
| 24. Mr. N. Macpherson | 50. Wing-Cdr. R. Grant-Ferris | 76. Mr. E. Partridge | 103. Mr. J. Ramsden | 129. Rt. Hon. E. Shinwell |
| 25. Mr. J. Godber | 51. Lt.-Colonel F. Hendry | 77. Sir Cuthbert Thornton-Kemsley | 104. Mr. M. Hughes-Young | 130. Rt. Hon. C. Ede |
| 26. Mr. A. Barber | 52. Mr. S. McMaster | 78. Lt.-Commander L. Maydon | 105. Rt. Hon. Sir H. Hylton-Foster | 131. Miss M. Herbison |
| | | 79. Sir Lionel Heald | | |

*The key to the painting by A.R. Thomson. My son Maurice, seated behind me*
*(No.33), was replying – the first time a father and son had done so this century.*
*(NB: Nos 6–18, 26, 63, 81, 84, 97, 98,*
*100, 108, 110, 113, 115, 117, 118, 128.)*

127

The opinion polls were cautiously encouraging, but Macmillan realised that the election would be won or lost on his own performance as party leader. He had until then made only two successful appearances on television – one with two American journalists and the other in conversation with Eisenhower, who had made a five-day visit to Britain in August and helped to emphasise his friend's new status as a world statesman. His party political broadcasts had been stilted, and he had to appear in another two days before the election. He brought in Norman Collins to advise him, and Collins devised a format for the broadcast that brought out the best in him. It was supplemented by an exhausting nationwide tour.

*Left and below right: Learning to perform in the unfamiliar medium of television. Professor Robert McKenzie (below) was later to become my 'television biographer' and a close friend.*

Above: *A stage on which I was more at home. All my elections were lost and won in the industrial heart of the country, such as here at Carlton in Nottinghamshire. I felt the strength of the support from ordinary working men who had indeed then 'never had it so good'.*

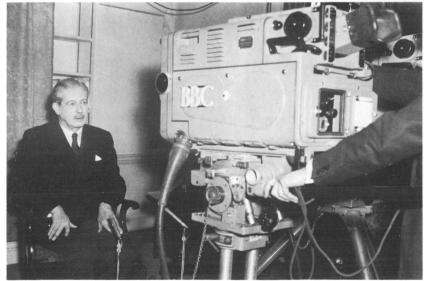

*Speaking for Joe Godber in Grantham in the 1959 Election. I have often wondered if by chance Mrs Margaret Thatcher was visiting her home town that day....*

The result – an overall Conservative majority of 100 – surpassed the wildest hopes of the party and 'Supermac' was born in folklore and cartoon. Not only had the public grown to respect his achievements as Prime Minister, they had also developed an affection for his personal style. Three days after the election, the man regarded by many as an Edwardian throw-back was writing in his diary: 'The great thing is to keep the Tory party on *modern* and *progressive* lines.'

*Supermac — as a cartoon hero at least — first appeared in 1959 and was still going strong in 1982.*

*On the campaign trail again, with Dorothy in Clapham in 1959.*

# The Prime Minister and the World

Macmillan was later to calculate that as Prime Minister he spent three-quarters of his time on foreign affairs – a reflection, to some extent, of his own priorities, for he was no little Englander. His most urgent challenge was the rise of black nationalism within the Commonwealth. Britain must respond positively, swiftly and generously to the widespread and accelerating demands in her colonies for independence and majority rule. Needless delay would generate bitterness and wreck his hopes for a Commonwealth of old colonies represented as free and equal partners.

He had seen at first hand de Gaulle's humiliation during his long struggle for recognition by the Allies, and was still living with the consequences. In analysing that episode he draws on Dr Johnson's famous letter to Lord Chesterfield: 'Patronage would have been welcome had it been timely.' He had no intention of repeating the mistakes of his predecessors; in seeking a Colonial Secretary in October 1959, he unhesitatingly chose a man 'of great imagination, even genius' – the radical Iain Macleod.

Macmillan and Macleod had to find the balance between a measured, gentle transition, and the human benefits of speed. Broadly, they favoured the latter. It was not that Macmillan had forgotten the lessons of India – that Britain should leave each colony with a constitutional settlement conducive to peaceful and democratic government – but he knew pragmatically that in some instances no guarantee of racial or tribal harmony was possible. Clinging on by force was no solution for the colonies, and at home the timing was right. He had a majority large enough to risk the alienation of his own right wing; his administration was at the beginning of its term; and he had the experience, courage and conviction to face the inevitable storms ahead.

*With Jack Kennedy outside the White House, April 1961. I enjoyed his company enormously.*

*The inevitable 'team' photograph: in Ghana, 1960. President and Mrs Nkrumah in front with Dorothy and me. In the back row on the left: Norman Brooke, later Secretary of the Cabinet; in the centre: John Wyndham, who had been with me since Algiers in 1940; and on the right in the striped tie: David Hunt, then Assistant Under-Secretary of State at the Commonwealth Relations Office, later to become 'Mastermind' and a neighbour in Sussex.*

Less than three months after the election, he set off for Africa. His 1958 Commonwealth tour had cemented links; this one would be 'mentally and morally' far more testing. His public speeches could not ignore the racial tensions that were convulsing the continent, yet every word would come under the closest scrutiny in the British and world press.

Between 5 January and 15 February 1960 Macmillan and Lady Dorothy covered almost 20,000 miles and visited Ghana, Nigeria, the Central African Federation (Southern and Northern Rhodesia and Nyasaland) and South Africa. He learned more about Africa's problems: Dr Nkrumah's ambitions for a one-party state; the tribalism of Nigeria that threatened its political unity; the wholly irreconcilable aspirations of the three constituent parts of the Central African Federation; and, most dispiriting of all, the complete inability of Dr Verwoerd to see any point of view other than his own. Nonetheless, he felt the power and promise of Africa, and grew more convinced that, however traumatic the handover might be, the peoples' right to determine their destinies could be neither denied nor delayed.

In South Africa he made his philosophy clear in a speech to the Houses of Parliament in Cape Town. He spoke of his new awareness of the strength of African national consciousness: 'The wind of change is blowing through this continent, and, whether we like it or not, this growth of national consciousness is a political fact. We must all accept it as a fact, and our national policies must take account of it.' Tipping his cap diplomatically to the white contribution to South Africa, he went on to reject on Britain's behalf 'the idea of the inherent superiority of one race over another'. After stressing that Britain, as a fellow-Commonwealth member, would like to offer support and encouragement, he added: 'I hope you won't mind my saying frankly that there are some aspects of your policies which make it impossible for us to do this without being false to our own deep convictions about the political destinies of free men to which in our own territories we are trying to give effect.'

This was probably the most important speech of Macmillan's life. The phrase 'wind of change' secured worldwide headlines, and his courage and frankness in facing the issue squarely in hostile territory won him admiration and trust that was of incalculable value in gaining the friendship of black Africa. Right-wing Tories formed the Monday Club to commemorate the 'Black Monday' on which the speech was made, but, try as they might, they brought about no deviation from the path he had chosen.

*Making the 'Wind of Change' speech to a joint meeting of 250 members of the Assembly and Senate of the South African Parliament in Cape Town, February 1960.*

Above: *The old Empire. A noisy and somewhat intimidating welcome to Goedgegun in Swaziland during the Commonwealth tour of January 1960.*

*I always seemed to acquire hats overseas. Left: At a goldmine in South Africa in 1960. Dorothy found the helmet invaluable at Birch Grove for tying up vulnerable shrubs at night when there was an unexpected late frost. Right: With Sir Roy Welensky, Prime Minister of the Rhodesian Federation, in Broken Hill, his constituency, in January 1960.*

*The impact of Muslim culture in Northern Nigeria vividly illustrated by charging horsemen, the traditional Jani, cultural cousins of the Tuareg. We visitors found them very exciting.*

**Below:** *The only way to get ashore in Accra was to be rowed through the waves in a surf boat – equally exciting; and they clearly didn't want us to get our feet wet.*

139

*With the South African Premier,
Dr Hendrik Verwoerd, at
Wynberg in February 1960. A
perfectly nice man, but with a
totally closed mind. He was
assassinated six years later.*

South Africa's intransigence eventually took her out of the Commonwealth in May 1961. Macmillan's grief was counter-balanced by
many gains. During the lifetime of the Conservative Government, new members of the Commonwealth included long-troubled
Cyprus, and Nigeria, Tanganyika, Uganda, Kenya and Zambia. The
talents of Macleod, Sandys and Butler contributed to a settlement in
the Central African Federation, dissolved without bloodshed in
December 1963. In the Caribbean, the West Indies Federation
proved unworkable and was dissolved, but Jamaica and Trinidad
and Tobago came into the Commonwealth as independent members.
(The advances were tarnished for Macmillan by the intrinsically
illiberal but politically necessary Commonwealth Immigrants Bill of
February 1962, which followed in the wake of the 1958 race riots and
a six-fold increase in immigration figures between 1959 and 1961.)

Though Macmillan relied greatly on the talents of his colleagues during the long and tortuous negotiations, he deserves credit for far more than visionary leadership. His rapport with individual political leaders and the assiduity with which he cultivated them were of enormous value in maintaining goodwill. He was himself involved in a series of brutally taxing conferences in which his persistence as a negotiator was exceeded only by his subtlety and skill. For all the setbacks and disappointments, Macmillan gave more to the Commonwealth than any Prime Minister before or since.

East–West relations were not forgotten. Patient work to arrange a meeting of heads of Government was bearing fruit by the time Macmillan won the election. After the success of Khrushchev's visit to the United States in September 1959, Eisenhower had at last grown enthusiastic about the Summit concept. He came to Paris in December for a successful meeting with Macmillan and de Gaulle, at which the Summit was fixed for the following May, in the hope of making it an annual event. And, at de Gaulle's insistence, it was agreed that tripartite meetings of Britain, France and the United States should be held with equal regularity. These developments were a source of great pride and hope to Macmillan. All his diplomatic dealings had taught him the value of face-to-face contact between allies or antagonists. He believed that Khrushchev genuinely wanted a compromise over Berlin and nuclear tests. In March Kruschchev suggested a test moratorium, and Macmillan persuaded Eisenhower to respond more warmly than the Pentagon recommended.

Until shortly before the Summit, Macmillan had every reason to be optimistic. The blow fell on 5 May, when Khrushchev announced that an American U2 had been shot down over Soviet territory, and Eisenhower soon made things worse by his naïve admission that he had known about espionage flights. Macmillan appreciated his friend's honesty and regretted his lack of guile.

Khrushchev came to the Summit on the attack. At the opening session he insulted Eisenhower, and demanded the postponement of discussions until after he had left office. Though Eisenhower showed dignified restraint and both de Gaulle and Macmillan were eloquent, the Summit was beyond saving and 'the grand edifice which I had worked so long and painfully to build seemed totally and finally destroyed'. The conference was abandoned the following day. Macmillan understood the reasons for Khrushchev's fury, but deplored his lack of statesmanship: 'A greater man would have made all the capital he could by his protests, but would have seized the opportunity to rise above his feelings of injury and thus shown himself the dominant figure in world politics. By his actual handling of the affair he lost a great opportunity – but so, alas, did the whole world.'

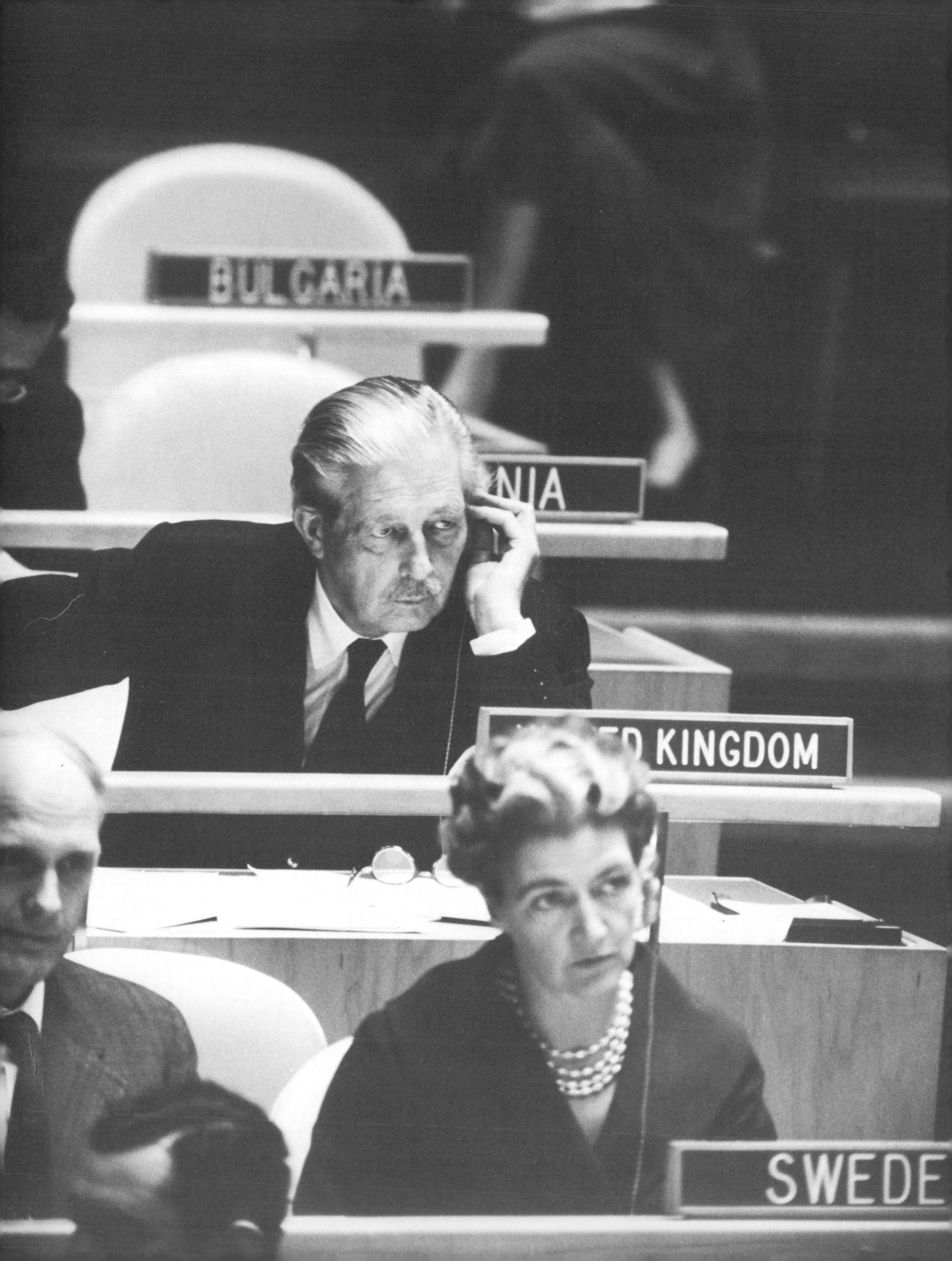
BULGARIA
NIA
KINGDOM
SWEDE

The recognition at home and abroad that Macmillan deserved no blame for the collapse of the Summit was of little consolation. He could only watch with pain a gradual deterioration in East–West relations over the ensuing months, made worse by the outbreak of trouble in the Congo in July.

The crisis in the Congo was to last until Katanga's bid for separation finally ended in December 1961. Britain was a strong supporter throughout of the United Nations policy of intervention to avert civil war but, though Macmillan played an important role as a mediator, his finest moment was early in the conflict when he came face to face with Khrushchev again. In September 1960, they both addressed the United Nations Assembly in New York. The Soviet leader delivered a three-hour harangue, designed for Afro-Asian consumption, against the UN. Macmillan countered with a moderate speech that did a great deal to lower the temperature, despite Khrushchev's loud interruptions, which culminated in his banging his shoe on the desk. After one such exhibition Macmillan stopped and said: 'Mr President, perhaps we could have a translation, I could not quite follow.' His domestic reputation for urbanity and unflappability was disseminated worldwide overnight.

John F. Kennedy succeeded Eisenhower in November 1960. As soon as the election results were announced, Macmillan wrote: 'I must somehow convince him that I am worth consulting not as an old friend (as Eisenhower felt) but as a man who, although of advancing years, has young and fresh thoughts.' To that end he spent much of the Christmas recess exercising 'that fatal itch for composition which is the outcome of a classical education' and preparing for Kennedy what became known as 'The Grand Design' – a paper on the main issues facing the West in 1961.

He had his reward in March, when he arrived in Trinidad on the first stage of a short tour of the West Indies: there he received a telegram from Kennedy pressing him to fly to Key West in Florida the following day for talks about Laos. 'I had never before been 1,800 miles to luncheon,' but Kennedy thought nothing of it. They disagreed on Laos, but an immediate spark was struck between them.

They built up a close, relaxed and deeply affectionate relationship based on a common sense of fun. Even as early as April 1961, an American journalist noted that Macmillan's follow-up visit to Washington was 'like a house-party and at times almost like a spree'. To Macmillan, Kennedy was a delightful change from the rather ponderous American politicians he was used to. For Kennedy, Macmillan's wit and sense of the ridiculous bridged the age-gap. They took a mutual delight in tormenting solemn colleagues with

*Listening to Wladyslaw Gomulka, head of the Polish Government from 1956 to 1970, at the United Nations, September 1960. The Soviets often tried out new tactics through their satellites, so the speech merited close attention.*

*To Prime Minister Harold Macmillan – who has "pointed the way" on this and many previous occasions – with high esteem and every good wish – John F. Kennedy – April 8, 1961.*

*'To Prime Minister Harold Macmillan – who has "pointed the way" on this and many previous occasions – with high esteem and every good wish – John F. Kennedy – April 8, 1961.' With Alec Home and Secretary of State Dean Rusk.*

occasional flights into frivolity, including a po-faced conversation about including Russia in the rotating NATO command. Links were strengthened by Macmillan's appointment – at Kennedy's request – of David Ormsby Gore (Lord Harlech from 1964) as British Ambassador to Washington. Gore was a close friend of Robert Kennedy and the brother-in-law of Maurice Macmillan, and he developed an unparalleled intimacy with the White House.

Their friendship developed yet further after Kennedy's unproductive and rather humiliating meetings in May and June with de Gaulle and Khrushchev. His subsequent visit to London made him realise how much he could gain from Macmillan's wisdom, wealth of experience and long view of international affairs. Typically, Macmillan was content to give Kennedy advice privately, making no public capital out of the influence he exerted on him. They could meet only rarely but they communicated frequently by other means, notably during the week of the Cuban crisis in October 1962. Macmillan had to live with accusations from opponents that the conduct of the United States disproved its 'special relationship' with Britain, while keeping it secret that Kennedy was ringing him up to three times daily to discuss his next move. When Macmillan resigned Kennedy wrote to him privately that 'we have never had a failure of understanding or of mutual trust. I believe that the world is a little more safe and the future of freedom more hopeful than when we began, and I am certain that history will recognise your great role in this improvement.' They last met at Birch Grove in July 1963.

*The rocking chair brought to Birch Grove for President Kennedy to ease the pain from the back injury acquired when his torpedo boat was sunk in the Second War. With typical propriety the Office of Works sent me a bill for the chair after my retirement.*

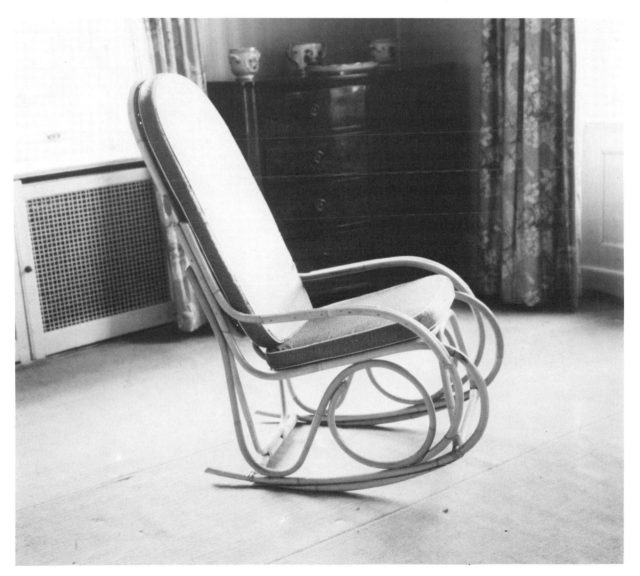

Of course there were differences between the two countries that might have soured the relationship. One such was Britain's quest for an independent nuclear deterrent. Having poured a great deal of effort and money into developing a weapon in the 1950s, the Government had decided in 1960 to cut its losses, abandon its latest project, Blue Streak, and put in its place Skybolt, the rocket then under development in the United States. US agreement to provide Skybolt was firm and there was a verbal assurance from Eisenhower that Polaris would be a substitute should Skybolt not be available.

In December 1962 Washington announced that Skybolt's future was uncertain, putting Macmillan in a highly embarrassing position at home. He flew to Nassau for pre-arranged talks with Kennedy. They had intended to discuss world issues. Instead the emphasis of the three days was on intense negotiations about Skybolt and Polaris,

*Birch Grove in June 1963, shortly before Jack Kennedy's visit. The house was built by my mother in 1926 and Dorothy created the garden.*

Above: *My sitting-room at the house, where talks with both de Gaulle and Jack Kennedy took place. On the chair is the Sargent drawing of my father.*

ending in a tremendous victory for Macmillan. Kennedy had grown to value his advice so much that he was prepared to ignore his advisers and give him what he wanted. Britain was promised Polaris missiles on the undemanding condition that she make them available to NATO except 'where supreme national interests are at stake'.

Less than a month later, Macmillan suffered the worst defeat of his career. In August 1961, Britain had formally applied to join the Common Market. Macmillan had come to accept that there was no prospect of persuading the French that the EEC should associate in any way with EFTA, and decided to go all out for membership of the EEC itself. He had spent considerable effort in courting the key figures – Adenauer and de Gaulle – in winning the backing of his own party and the British public, and in neutralising the opposition of the Commonwealth to Britain's membership. He sensed that de Gaulle was fundamentally opposed because of his suspicions of Britain's closeness to the United States and a fear that she would compete with

147

FRANKLIN

MAC'S NEW SUMMIT CLIMB
UNFAVOURABLE REACTION FROM FRANCE & GERMANY EXPECTED

"QUICK! GET THE SOOTHING LOTION——THE OLD FEET ARE KILLING ME AGAIN "

*The painful path to the political summit when I tried to take Britain into Europe.*

France for leadership of the EEC. Yet de Gaulle raised no objection in principle to the British application. Macmillan's guess was that he was gambling on the Tory Party or the Commonwealth to do the job for him. In the event, through the political acumen of Macmillan and the negotiating skills of Edward Heath, the last difficulties were ironed out by the end of 1962, to the satisfaction of all but de Gaulle. On 14 January he exercised his veto to prevent Britain's entry.

It was a shattering blow to Macmillan. 'We have lost everything,' he wrote in his diary, 'except our courage and determination.' He was too disciplined to give way to despair. Within a couple of months he turned to another issue which had concerned him for a long time – nuclear tests.

The dangers of uncontrolled atmospheric tests had led to public protests as well as deep worry for Macmillan personally. For years he had seized every opportunity to press for a ban, only to be thwarted by some crisis in East–West relations. Now, in March 1963, on hearing that the latest round of disarmament talks in Geneva had reached deadlock, he decided on another initiative. Khrushchev was prepared to consider a ban backed up by some method of international inspection. Macmillan wrote to Kennedy outlining a possible basis for a treaty. Kennedy agreed with the terms and they wrote jointly offering to send senior representatives to Moscow for discussions; in July Averell Harriman and Lord Hailsham were on their way.

'I have learned,' wrote Macmillan later, 'that in all negotiations nothing matters except the will to reach agreement.' This time the will was there on the three sides, and Macmillan contributed not just British acquiescence, but his persuasion of Kennedy to ignore the advisers and concede minor issues for the sake of securing the principle. It was Macmillan, too, who had picked the right time and found the right mechanism. When he heard from Kennedy on 25 July that the United States had initialled the treaty, 'I had to go out of the room. I went to tell D. and burst into tears.' He had worked, pleaded, cajoled and prayed for this outcome for years, and even the Opposition and the press regarded it as a triumph. He had succeeded with the Commonwealth, the Anglo-American relationship and Polaris. He had failed with the Summit and the EEC. It was fitting that this achievement was to be the last major foreign policy initiative of his Prime Ministership.

# The Prime Minister at Home

'Let's be frank about it; most of our people have never had it so good
... What is beginning to worry some of us is "Is it too good to be
true?" or perhaps I should say "Is it too good to last?" ... Can we
control inflation? This is the problem of our time.'

This passage from a thoughtful speech in June 1957 attracted little
attention at the time. It was some years before a phrase was wrenched
out of context and distorted. Macmillan was accused of appealing to
the basest instincts of the electorate with the phrase 'You've never
had it so good'. In the early 1960s, this tag was used to ridicule and
denigrate him for materialism and lack of spirituality. He was particularly wounded when it formed the basis for attacks in a sermon
from the Archbishop of Canterbury and a speech from Lord Salisbury. Later, he was to be pilloried along with other figureheads of the
'Thirteen Years of Tory Misrule' for having cynically permitted an
import boom. And in the 1970s monetarists blamed him for failing
to cut public expenditure just when the nation was beginning to live
beyond its means.

These are heavy charges. In fact Macmillan was a materialist in so
far as he wanted, like Disraeli, 'improvement in the well-being of the
people', and set his face against unemployment, which he
abominated both as a human tragedy and a waste of resources. He
did unleash a boom of unexpected proportions in the pre-election
budget, with adverse effects on inflation and the balance of payments, but he took action to correct it immediately afterwards. Ever
alive to the need to 'square the circle' of a positive balance of payments, full employment and low inflation, like his successors he
could usually meet only one, or at the most two, of the three criteria.
And as a Keynesian by nature and training, when he made errors he
made them in the direction of expansion.

*On a visit to the rebuilt Coventry Cathedral after my resignation: leaving the fire-blackened shell of the old cathedral destroyed by German bombs during the Second War and left as a sort of quad outside Sir Basil Spence's splendid new building.*

151

*The Lord Mayor's Banquet, an annual opportunity to speak to the city and, through television, to the country, shortly after the Opening of Parliament. On this occasion, in November 1958, others on the top table included Rab, then Home Secretary; the Archbishop of Canterbury, Dr Fisher; the visiting Lord Mayor, Sir Denis Truscott; the New Lord Mayor, Sir Harold Gillett; and David Kilmuir, the Lord Chancellor.*

*With Walter Monckton at the Eton and Harrow match at Lord's in July 1960. Close colleagues and friends for many years, we were on this occasion implacable rivals, Walter being an Old Harrovian!*

Despite the Macmillan Government's reputation for profligacy and irresponsibility, he had realised earlier than most that the key problem in British industry was low productivity and its failure to rise in line with wage settlements. It was to securing realistic wage settlements and encouraging industrial modernisation that Macmillan was committed from 1960 onwards. He and Selwyn Lloyd (Chancellor from July 1960) launched the National Economic Development Council in the summer of 1961 to assist with economic and industrial planning. They also introduced the Pay Pause of 1961–1962, which with all its inevitable unfairnesses and breaches was a necessary stage in combatting the economy's central problem. And it was Macmillan himself who provided most of the inspiration and hard work behind the devising of the pioneering National Incomes Commission. Complementary to those long-term measures was the EEC application, for Macmillan hoped for an enlargement in the export market to stimulate economic growth. The General's veto was as damaging to economic as to foreign policy.

Inevitably, political opponents and the media concentrated on the short-term economic problems of his period in office: runs on reserves, sudden jumps in imports and all the other indicators of trouble ahead. Yet by comparison with more recent years, Macmillan presided over an extremely healthy economy. With work proceeding on his long-term strategies, he felt it unnecessary to do more than alternate – as circumstances dictated – between the brake and the accelerator. This fine-tuning became known as Selwyn Lloyd's 'Stop-Go' policy and encountered much scorn and derision.

The major failing of these economic policies was in their presentation. Lloyd was a conscientious Chancellor, but he had not the knack of selling his budgets or interim measures positively. Coupled to that, he lacked imagination or energy to do more than deal with problems as they arose and long-term thinking fell to Macmillan. The fact of the matter, as he noted frequently in his diaries, was that the older members of the Government were tired. Eight new Ministers had been brought into his post-election Cabinet, but too many senior Ministers had endured the strain of major office since 1951. He was often tired himself, for the demands of his innovative approach to foreign policy were an appalling burden on a man in his late sixties, suffering still from the effects of the old war wound and occasional attacks of gout. Yet his spirit was still young and his instincts radical, and faced by a deterioration in the fortunes of the Tory Party at a series of by-elections, he determined to give the Government a new image. He had appointed Iain Macleod to the Chairmanship of the party in October 1961 with a view to disseminating 'Progressive Toryism'. Some months later – partially as a consequence of pressure from Butler and Macleod – he became convinced that there would have to be a Government reshuffle too.

It was Lloyd's failure that precipitated the reshuffle, but it ended in a public relations catastrophe. Macmillan could have achieved his purpose by replacing Lloyd and making minor Cabinet changes later. Instead he sought to mask Lloyd's dismissal by carrying out a major purge. In July 1962 he announced the removal of one-third of the Cabinet and eight other Ministers and created one of the youngest Cabinets of the century. Overnight, he became 'MAC THE KNIFE'. What had been intended as a sign of invigoration was interpreted as a panic measure – the 'JULY MASSACRE'.

Macmillan was the victim of his party's success in staying so long in office. As he had observed astutely in his diary in November 1961, 'the public were becoming bored with the party and the party bored with itself'. This boredom was reflected in the press, which dramatised every set-back as additional proof that Macmillan had lost his grip. And the Opposition harped incessantly on his age. In

*The school photograph, Chequers 1963. Judging by their expressions most of the boys have good reports.*
  *Back row: Michael Noble: Julian Amery; Aubrey Jones; Jack Profumo; Tim Bligh; unidentified; Michael Fraser; Knox Cunningham; Freddy Erroll: Geoffrey Rippon; Keith Joseph; Richard Wood.*
  *Middle row: Peter Carrington; Christopher Soames; Edward Heath; Jack Maclay; Edward Boyle; Peter Thorneycroft; Hugh Fraser; unidentified; John Boyd-Carpenter; Bill Deedes.*
  *Front row: Enoch Powell; Ernest Marples; Iain Macleod; Henry Brooke; Rab; self; Reggie Maudling; unidentified; Reggie Manningham-Buller; Quintin Hailsham.*

Right: *The group breaking up,
with Quintin's back to the camera.
I seem to have missed the joke,
which was clearly a good one.*

November 1961 Michael Foot attacked him in the House as a 'petulant and pathetic old man'.

Much foreign travel did take its toll. There were periods when Macmillan seemed very tired; he failed to speak enough in the House and when he did sometimes spoke badly. Yet he continued to confound his critics by frequently bouncing back to the top of his form, and the headlines would announce the return of 'Supermac'. 'One must get used to being lauded one day and defamed the next,' he wrote later. 'Perhaps the most trying experience is being preached at. But all this is part of the game.' *The Times* was the paper that most offended by preaching. Macmillan had never forgotten the paper's devout support for appeasement and found its advice and magisterial denunciations hard to bear during his Prime Ministership. Yet it did perform for him one signal service – over the election for the Chancellorship of Oxford University in 1960, an office which he still carries out with particular delight.

*A Prime Minister, unlike a prophet, is not without honour in his own country. My election as Chancellor of Oxford University caused some fluttering in the academic dovecotes, but all was happily settled by the installation in 1960. My grandson Alexander was my page.*

Of all the experiences of his period of office, his fight for election as Chancellor gave him the simplest, most unadulterated pleasure. It was master-minded by Hugh Trevor-Roper, who took exception in the spring of 1960 to Sir Maurice Bowra's attempt to push through unopposed the nomination of Sir Oliver Franks. Trevor-Roper considered Franks a dull choice and, searching for a candidate of distinction, scholarship and panache, came up with the name of the Prime Minister. He and the conspirators he gathered calculated that Macmillan 'would relish the idea of being the anti-establishment candidate'. The Cabinet saw things differently and advised the Prime Minister not to risk his political neck for something that did not merit it – to which Macmillan allegedly replied, 'like fox-hunting'. It was a close-run thing, but Macmillan was to admit to having enjoyed 'one unforeseen and perhaps decisive advantage' – a particularly pompous leader in *The Times* enjoining Oxford MAs to vote for Franks. Those arriving at the polling-station were confronted by a banner reading 'A vote for Franks is a vote for Sir William Haley', and the delighted Macmillan won by 280 votes.

He was delighted, too, to be made a Freeman of the City of London in December 1961, but there were few such undiluted pleasures

*In December 1961 the City of London honoured me with the Freedom of the City. Despite one of the last smogs, the coach-load of staff and tenants from Birch Grove made it to the Guildhall as did some twenty members of my family.*

*LOOKING AHEAD!*

Above: *Autumn 1961: the rebuilding of No. 10 was in full swing. Looking across from Admiralty House, our temporary home on the other side of Horse Guards, progress seemed painfully slow.*

Right: *Winston leaving Admiralty House on 8 March 1961, one of the last occasions on which we entertained him.*

during his period in office. For the most part, it was an exhausting daily grind of unrelentingly hard work, a total absence of privacy and a loneliness that was relieved only by his family and his personal staff. He did not even have the comfort of living at No. 10, for from August 1960 to September 1963 it had to be rebuilt and the Macmillans and their entourage moved to the less homely Admiralty House. Nevertheless, though Macmillan occasionally in bleak moments contemplated resignation, he found being Prime Minister 'great fun'. As he says reasonably in his memoirs, no one has any sympathy with the self-pitying statesman. 'After all, the answer is easy. Nobody asked you to hold up the world. If your shoulders are tired, there are others ready and anxious to sustain the burden.'

Macmillan would happily have sustained the burden at least until after the next election. In the event, a series of security scandals wore him down and left him disinclined to surmount the ill health that finally precipitated his resignation. In 1961 there were the trials and convictions of the Portland Bill spies and George Blake; in 1962 the Vassall case brought to light titillating details of blackmail and homosexuality and a Government Minister, Tam Galbraith, was smeared by innuendo; and in February 1963 rumours began to circulate about the link between the Secretary of State for War, John Profumo, a call-girl, Christine Keeler, and the Soviet Naval Attaché, Captain Ivanov.

*Wondering if we are late for church. Autumn 1960, with my granddaughter Rachel Macmillan and Dorothy following behind.*

Left: *An improbable picture, organised for the benefit of the BBC at Birch Grove in February 1963. Dorothy, Maurice and his son Alexander are pushing the sledge carrying Leo and Elizabeth Amery and, hidden, Rachel Macmillan.*

*The grouse moor again.* Left: *At Bolton in 1960. Left to right: Tom Egerton; Hugh Fraser; Martyn Beckett; Andrew and Debo (Devonshire); self; and Mr More-O'Farrell.* Right: *September 1960, with Dorothy in a butt at Swinton in Lancashire.*

Below: *At Lord's for the Eton and Harrow match in July 1963, with my daughter Carol Faber, behind me in the dark glasses, watching her son Michael batting for the Eton XI.*

161

162

Had Macmillan not reluctantly accepted Galbraith's resignation only to see him vindicated by a tribunal of enquiry, he might have been more sceptical about Profumo's protestations of innocence. Had two journalists not been sent to prison for failing to disclose their sources on Galbraith, the media might not have been so anxious to excoriate the Macmillan Government and exploit the Profumo story. And had the satire wave not begun in 1962 with *Private Eye*, *Beyond the Fringe* and *That Was the Week That Was*, the temptation to focus the whole scandal on to the instantly recognisable Edwardian at the head of the Government would have been less strong. It was Macmillan's very image of old-fashioned probity that lent incongruity and a delicious *frisson* to the whole Profumo affair. The time was ripe, Macmillan reflected later, for a sacrifice to the gods. 'What could be a more convenient victim for this purpose than an elderly but respectable Conservative Prime Minister?'

It is true that Macmillan was not equipped to deal lightly with the sexual scandal that broke when, in June, Profumo admitted his relationship with Keeler. His knowledge of human nature was considerable, but his assumptions about colleagues did not include the possibility that they might move in such circles as Profumo did, or compromise their honour by lying. During the following months, although his health had been affected by the trauma, his primary concern was not to be driven out of office on a 'flood of filth'. He felt that the media reaction to the Profumo disclosures cloaked a desire to pull down the establishment. To a friendly interviewer he said in July of his unwillingness to resign: 'I wasn't going to have the British Government pulled down by the antics of a whore.'

During the summer he had some respite from such miseries. His role in securing the Test Ban Treaty had been acknowledged as a triumph by the press and had revived his reputation. There followed a few weeks in Finland and Sweden with Lady Dorothy that, though partly official, included plenty of time for relaxation. Then he had ten days shooting in England. He had to make a decision about his future, for he must either retire soon or lead the party into a General Election. In September and October he had many consultations with colleagues and changed his mind on several occasions. He betrayed a wholly uncharacteristic indecisiveness and need for reassurance, symptoms of the illness that was to strike him down with brutal suddenness. On 7 October he finally made up his mind to stay on as Prime Minister. Twenty-four hours later he was in King Edward VII Hospital awaiting an urgent operation for a serious inflammation of the prostate gland, and preparing to send the Queen his resignation.

*The much anticipated annual visit to Bolton Abbey, with my hostess Debo, the Duchess of Devonshire, and her daughter Sophie in September 1961.*

# Elder Statesman

Macmillan's operation was on 10 October; he resigned formally eight days later. In between, the Tory Party conference at Blackpool was conducted in a near-hysterical atmosphere of intrigue. As he reflected later, 'Political death is always uncomfortable; but in my case it could not have been more untimely.' Knowing that Macmillan intended to resign, and that the succession was wide open, the party, the media and the betting-shops had a field day.

The unfortunate Rab Butler, again acting PM, was once more the obvious favourite. He was brought down by three major factors: he was not a popular conference performer; he lacked ruthlessness; and, most important, Macmillan was determined even from his sick-bed to ensure that he was succeeded by a 'swordsman' rather than a 'gownsman'. Butler had 'a fine, academic mind' but he had neither the decisiveness nor the inspirational qualities that Macmillan thought necessary to win an election and lead the country with honour. Butler was a reformer; Macmillan was a radical. There is a world of difference. It is significant that Butler's hero was the worthy Sir Robert Peel, while Macmillan venerated the great adventurers – Disraeli, Lloyd George and Churchill.

Macmillan's first choices were Hailsham and Macleod, 'the men of real genius in the party who were the true inheritors of the Disraeli tradition of Tory Radicalism'. When neither proved to be in with a chance, Macmillan settled for Lord Home, for whose performance as Foreign Secretary he had the deepest admiration. His pedigree was in his favour, for Macmillan had never lost his respect for the aristocratic tradition of honourable public service.

There have been many disputes about the extent of Macmillan's influence on the 'magic circle' that finally chose Home as the man most likely to unite the party. What is certain is that his wishes were known and carried weight and that, by brilliant timing of his official resignation, he nipped in the bud a revolt by the pro-Butler faction. It was a gamble that almost came off: after thirteen years in Government the Tories came within a whisker of winning the 1964 election. That they did not was a consequence of the boredom factor and the brilliant showmanship of Harold Wilson.

*September 1973. With Harold Wilson, at a reception at the Dorchester to mark the publication of my final volume of memoirs.*

165

*Reading has always been one of my greatest pleasures.*

*This picture was taken in the garden at Birch Grove after my retirement from office.*

For Macmillan initially the hardest part of leaving office was the ending of his close working relationship with the Queen. They were genuinely fond of each other. She had greatly impressed him with her conscientiousness and grasp of detail, and the courage and devotion she displayed in helping to keep the Commonwealth together. For her, Macmillan had proved a welcome relief after the overpowering Churchill and the nervous Eden. 'For the greater part of my reign,' she wrote to him '. . . you have been my guide and supporter through the mazes of international affairs and my instructor in many vital matters relating to our constitution and to the political and social life of my people. There is therefore no question of your successor, however admirable he may be, being able to perform exactly those services which you have given so generously and for which I am so deeply grateful.'

Like many of his friends, she hoped he would take an earldom. But given Macmillan's respect for the true aristocracy, there was no chance of his joining those he thought 'jumped-up'. A hereditary title would in any case have been incongruous for the man who had introduced life-peerages, and a life-peerage would have been even further beneath his dignity. He had no desire to participate in public life from amid the ranks of failed and retired politicians. His wife was given a DBE in January 1964 in recognition of her indefatigable charity work. The only honour he was prepared to accept from the Queen was the OM, which he received in 1976. It was a fitting tribute to the Macmillan heritage.

He did not retire from the House of Commons until the General Election. He spoke only three more times, and in melancholy circumstances: once about the Denning Report on the Profumo affair; once in great grief after the assassination of John Kennedy; and most poignantly of all, in July 1964 after the death of Churchill, whom he had admired and loved as no other man in public life and to whom he had been attentive and affectionate throughout his last years.

He was determined to stay out of politics – 'it has always seemed to me more artistic, when the curtain falls on the last performance, to accept the inevitable *E finita la commedia*. It is tempting, perhaps, but unrewarding to hang about the greenroom after final retirement from the stage.' It was a resolution to which he held rigidly for many years, tempted though he was in 1965 at a time of national crisis to offer himself for the leadership of a National Government. He had gone into retirement as a sick old man with no more to give. Within

*The only honour that appealed to me was the Order of Merit, which remains the Sovereign's personal gift. In November 1977, after a service in St James's Chapel, the members of the Order were entertained to lunch at the Palace.*

*Standing, left to right: Lord Todd; J. B. Priestley; Lord Hinton; Sir Alan Hodgkin; Sir George Edwards; Lord Penney; Sir Isaiah Berlin; self; Lord Clark; Sir Ronald Syme; Sir Freddy Ashton; Lord Franks.*

*Seated, left to right: Dame Veronica Wedgwood; Sir William Walton; Professor Dorothy Hodgkin; Graham Sutherland; The Queen; Prince Philip; Henry Moore; Lord Mountbatten; Lord Zuckerman; and Malcolm MacDonald.*

*At home, alone, after Dorothy's death.*

Opposite: *I hoped that I wasn't expected to eat this gift from a priest at the opening of a new Macmillan branch office in Madras, February 1976. The office was decorated for my visit, and I particularly liked the pillars featuring piles of books.*

a few months his health was much better and he found retirement dreary; his brain was still sharp and his wish to be of use unabated. He was left sad and lonely by Lady Dorothy's death in 1966.

He was greatly fortunate in having several occupations open to him. The first was the reorganisation of the publishing house of Macmillan, a process which had been initiated by his son Maurice following Daniel's retirement a few years earlier. For four years from 1963 Macmillan was Chairman and during that time he took monumental expansionist gambles in re-staffing, re-location and rationalisation that brought the firm leaping back to prosperity. Maurice then replaced him, but when he again became a Minister in 1970 (for obvious reasons, he had not achieved office until Home became Prime Minister), Macmillan took over again in partnership with his grandson, Alexander, until 1974. Maurice then became Chairman and Macmillan President. He still takes a considerable interest in the firm and is consulted on major policy decisions.

He has taken great pleasure from his incumbency of the Chan-cellorship of Oxford, a splendid retirement job for a man who enjoys intelligent company, gossip and nostalgic ceremony. He visits frequently, presents honorary degrees and presides and speaks on formal occasions. His idiosyncratic pronunciation of Latin gives an added delight to the most solemn ceremonies. As Chancellor he has been both useful and ornamental and even at eighty-nine is con-sidered by the majority of dons, alumni and undergraduates to be irreplaceable. He saw off in typical form a suggestion by a few young dons that it was time for a change, telling them that he would be quite prepared to stand down, but only for an older and wiser man.

Extensive foreign travel has also proved a diversion. His many trips abroad have included one to the United States on which he raised £50,000 for the Oxford Union and a visit to China in 1979 to investigate the Chinese book market. At home, much of his time is

necessarily spent in relative solitude at Birch Grove, where he now has a bed-sitting room in the bedroom he occupied from 1926. Yet he still travels to London quite frequently, using the free pass awarded to directors of the Great Western Railway when it was nationalised in 1947.

In his time he has been a member of seven clubs – the Atheneum, Beefsteak, Bucks, Carlton, Guards, Pratt's and Turf – and his frequent lunch and dinner visits are still valued by cronies of all ages, who relish his exquisite wit and masterly conversation. He was a highly effective Chairman of the Carlton from 1977 to 1979, and his legendary skills as a negotiator were of great use in bringing about a merger with the Junior Carlton. The club's gratitude to their most famous member was symbolised by their creation for him of the office of President for Life.

Most important of all his recent activities has been the writing of his six long volumes of autobiography. In giving him an opportunity to reflect and comment on the twentieth century, they slaked his thirst for political life. They were followed by *The Past Masters*, individual and thoughtful studies of his twentieth-century predecessors as Prime Minister.

*Hard at work on the memoirs. The library and Birch Grove were filled with boxes, filing cabinets and papers. The six volumes, totalling two million words, took eight years to complete.*

Below: *On a promotional tour of the US for the memoirs in January 1968, I paid a call on President Johnson with Pat Dean, our Ambassador in Washington: he offered us lunch – hamburgers!*

It cannot be a coincidence that Macmillan tiptoed back onto the political stage once he had finished writing about the past. From 1975, he found his active mind untaxed by any major work. The following year he gave an important television interview to Robin Day on 'Britain in Crisis', discussing the imbalance of Soviet and Western military strength and the serious economic crisis at home presaged by the shrinkage of the wealth-producing sector. He advocated the establishment of a broadly based National Government to take the unpopular measures necessary to redress the balance. He was giving serious contemplation to standing himself as a National candidate, but his plan was yet half-formed when the IMF loan and the stringent conditions attached to it brought the nation back from the brink of collapse.

During subsequent years, he has had to come to terms with a Conservative Prime Minister who has taken even more radical measures than he would have been prepared to advocate. Stockton memories have made him unhappy with the present level of unemployment, yet he has come to admire his successor's 'swordsman' qualities. Although Macmillan had little experience of working with women other than secretaries, he was not as appalled as might have been expected by Thatcher's election to the party leadership. At the Ministry of Housing he had been deeply impressed by Evelyn Sharp's intellect and commitment, and marked his approval by conferring on her an honorary doctorate from Oxford in his first exercise of patronage as Chancellor. When he unveiled a bust of Thatcher at the Carlton in 1979 he glanced round the portraits of former party leaders and reflected that 'some of them would have been glad, some would have been sorry – but not Disraeli, who preferred the ladies – all would have been surprised'. Although he likes on occasion to play the old fogey, Macmillan is no more rattled by change than he ever was.

His ability to look forward with a radical vision is remarkable. Since 1979 his political pronouncements have become more frequent, both in television interviews – most notably with Robert McKenzie – and in public speeches. He has called for 'revolution by consent' between industry and the trade unions, and for unity and stout resistance to the Soviet threat. His vision of a Europe united by a common defence, foreign and monetary policy has had Young Conservatives on their feet cheering for five minutes, and he has appeared on an election platform in support of a Tory candidate for the European Parliament. The content of his speeches has been both of the highest intellectual quality and impeccably concerned with principle rather than personalities. A tribute from a 1979 *Daily Telegraph* leader is as true today as when it was written.

*One of the sadnesses of living to a great age is the increasing loneliness. Leaving the Abbey after Rab's Memorial Service with two other ex-Prime Ministers, Harold Wilson and James Callaghan. I rather agree with Ralph Richardson that Memorial Services are the 'cocktail parties of the geriatric set'.*

Where all will agree is perhaps in finding in the Macmillan of the last 15 years a certain irresistible ripeness and charm. So many great men seem to have not the foggiest idea of how to behave when bereft of power. They obtrude or recede too much, embarrass or ignore their successors, offer help or advise when it is not required but not when it is. In his own retirement Mr Macmillan has achieved a sort of perfection: like the shaving soap, not too much or too little but just right, never officious or boring, without rancour or spite, always good-mannered and good-humoured, never despairing, always constructive alike in hope or warning. And of course, as all who saw him on television the other day will know, he is inspiring testimony to the fact that a man may endure all the successive strains of war and ill health and high office and old age and still retain unimpaired all his style and wit.

Oxford. Above: *The diptych by Bryan Organ, 1980, which now hangs in the University offices. The University commissioned it to commemorate my twenty years as Chancellor. Below: The procession from the Sheldonian Theatre after encaenia, the annual commemoration of founders and benefactors.*

*Four generations of the family together with my son Maurice at his home, Highgrove, at Christmas 1974. My grandson Alexander brought my first Macmillan great-grandson to see me.*

*Elizabeth R 1981*

The Privy Council meeting at which the engagement of the Prince of Wales was announced.

Back row - left to right: Sir Neville Leigh, Clerk of the Council; Lord Adeane; Nicholas Edwards, Secretary of State for Wales; Lord Charteris, Provost of Eton; Sir Harold Wilson; Lord Maclean, the Lord Chamberlain; Mr Michael Foot, the Leader of the Opposition; Lord Home; Mr William Whitelaw, Home Secretary; Ratu Sir Kamisese Hara, Prime Minister of Fiji; Sir Ian Gilmour, then Lord Privy Seal; Mr David Steel, Leader of the Liberal Party; Mr Humphrey Atkins, then Northern Ireland Secretary; Mr Donald Stewart, Leader of the Parliamentary Scottish National Party; Mr Milton Cato, Prime Minister of St Vincent and the Grenadines; Mr Douglas Anthony, then Deputy Prime Minister of Australia; Sir William Douglas, Chief Justice of Barbados; Sir Philip Moore, Private Secretary to the Queen; and Mr David Thomson, Leader of the House of Representatives of New Zealand.

Front row - left to right: Self; the Prime Minister; Dr Robert Runcie, the Archbishop of Canterbury; The Prince of Wales; The Queen; Lord Soames, then Lord President of the Council; Lord Hailsham, Lord Chancellor; Mr George Thomas, Speaker of the House of Commons; and Sir Seewoosagur Ramgoolam, Prime Minister of Mauritius.

Charles.

# *Epilogue:*
# The Actor-Manager

'Macmillan's role as a poseur was itself a pose,' concluded Harold Wilson in 1973. Many observers have been less shrewd. Recognising that he has been an actor all his public life, they have fallen into the trap of assuming that in everything he says or does he is merely playing a part. Nothing could be further from the truth. Macmillan has gradually adopted a style that cloaks a serious mind, passionate convictions and an inner privacy that no one is permitted to breach. In the Mediterranean he achieved power by pretending not to want it. In Opposition he accentuated his 'grouse-moor' image the more easily to seduce the party into left-wing policies. As Minister for Housing he brought about a revolution, but made it less alarming by his old-world courtesy. As Prime Minister, he led from the left and placated the right by his avuncular image and by emphasising his aristocratic links and respect for the symbols of an earlier age. He wooed the public by a skilful use of humour and an accentuation of his eccentricities. And now, in old age, he assumes an appearance of exaggerated frailty in order to point up the contrast with the freshness of his ideas. He has always been an actor–manager, determined to steer his enterprise to safety and prosperity.

A few have spotted the hard work behind the pretended dilettantism; the patient effort put into making his television appearances seem unrehearsed; the shuffling walk on the inevitable stick that turns in absent-minded moments into an unaided briskness; the effective theatricality of the notes he peers at when a point is emphasised, and which turn out to be extraneous if not actually blank – stage properties.

*At the Derby in 1972 in my seventy-ninth year. I always preferred the Derby to Ascot.*

175

*With my own eyesight failing, I have become more involved with the work of the Royal National Institute for the Blind, and in October 1982 visited Braille House in London to 'start the presses' on a new braille printing machine. This young lady, six-year-old Sarah Allen, herself visually handicapped and a pupil at the Sunshine Nursery School in East Grinstead near my home, made me feel most welcome.*

Yet little of the style is hollow; it is rather inspired type-casting of himself – an exaggeration of existing characteristics. The affection for the manners of by-gone years, the country pursuits, the courtesy, the puritanism – all these are genuine. When he puts on his Guards' tie, it is to remind himself of the values it represents. And behind the style lies a man whose intellect and deep sensitivity to a series of fearful experiences made him one of the most radical politicians of this century.

Macmillan has ever been intrigued by the turns of fate that dictate one's life: the war that taught him discipline and revealed his capacity for leadership; the wound that probably saved his life; the ill health that sent him to Ottawa rather than Bombay; the chance that sent him to Stockton; the lucky appointment to North Africa that tested and proved his capacity for diplomacy at the highest level; the ill-conceived and arbitrary housing commitment that made his name politically; the cruel bad luck of Anthony Eden that made him Prime Minister; and the equally harsh fortune that took the office from him before he was ready to quit the field.

It is his very understanding of the arbitrariness of fate that has prevented him from ever taking himself too seriously. He has a sense of history and an interest in people unique among senior politicians; nor does his sense of the absurdity of life detract from his fundamental seriousness. He sees what is ridiculous in himself and others while adhering to the chief principle – purposeful use of one's talents for the betterment of mankind. In his dealings with the eminent of many nations, much of his success has sprung from the fact that *he* made the concessions in what he would consider the least important area – personal aggrandisement. His objectives in the exercise of power have been strongly held. His behaviour as a public man has been affected by the knowledge that, at the superficial level, politics is a game. His memoirs show a detached appreciation of the tactics of his political opponents whom he judges like sportsmen, or actors like himself. When the performance is over and the participants have left the arena, he claps or boos as they deserve. It comes as no shock to him that a Labour Opposition should savage his Immigration Act for illiberality only to make it harsher when they reached office. The exercise of power has nothing to do with the frivolity of public debate.

About certain things his temperament and his experience have made him deadly earnest: the need to stand up to aggressors; the duty to the weak; the importance of maintaining the values of Western civilisation. All these principles come together in his belief that European unity is the prerequisite for survival. Reporting on a speech he gave in 1981 to the Conservative Group for Europe, David Wood of *The Times* began:

> Who was the raving internationalist or perhaps the callow visionary speaking a day or two ago the words that follow? 'Europe should have a united foreign policy, a united monetary policy, and treat itself as really one nation to resist the dangers with which it is threatened. In that way, however great may be the appeal to old-fashioned people of old-fashioned ideas, however great may be the appeal to patriotic people of the old patriotisms of the past – all that must sink to a common unity before a greater danger and to a common purpose to increase the prosperity and happiness of our people and to do two things: to create a modern civilisation and then to be determined to defend it to the end.' . . . When he took his bow and doddered from the room he left his audience with the ashes of their conviction fanned into brighter flame.

It is the vision of the old radical, at a time when politicians seem preoccupied by minutiae, that appeals to the young. In a lecture he gave to the Carlton Club in October 1982, after a masterly review of the history of civilisation that came from a life-time's reading, reflection and experience, he addressed himself to a future full of challenge, particularly that of using increased leisure to make the world a better place.

If I were 18 not 88 I would not be depressed. I would not think the game's up. I would not read or write nostalgic stories about how jolly the past was. It's a marvellous, wonderful picture that opens up . . . we are in one of those crises of civilisation which, if it faces it, can create a great new period of wealth and strength. If it shrinks from it, it will gradually decay and become out of date and some other peoples, perhaps whose civilisations have been long stagnant, will rise and take our place. That is the choice that lies before the youth, the middle-aged and the governing classes of every nation, but before they make it they must face the truth and not content themselves with just repeating the old slogans that we learnt and repeated over and over again 30 or 40 years ago.

The freshness, the vision and the courage are undimmed.

*In October 1982 the Carlton Club, of which I had been Chairman and more latterly President, celebrated its 150th anniversary. I gave the inaugural Carlton Lecture, organised by Lord Plummer, Chairman of the Political Committee and former Leader of the Greater London Council. My words were gratifyingly well received.*

# Bibliographical Note

Harold Macmillan's six volumes of autobiography (*Winds of Change 1914–1939, The Blast of War 1939–1945, Tides of Fortune 1945–1955, Riding the Storm 1956–1959, Pointing the Way 1959–1961* and *At the End of the Day 1961–1963*) were all published by his firm between 1966 and 1973. Although they reflect his reserve in their scanty treatment of his private life, they are imbued with insight and humour and far above the common run of political memoirs.

His vignettes of earlier Prime Ministers, *The Past Masters* (Macmillan, 1975), are illuminating, perceptive and highly readable.

Anthony Sampson's *Macmillan* (Allen Lane, 1967) still commands respect for its authoritative analysis. George Hutchinson's *The Last Edwardian at No. 10* (Quartet, 1980) is a detailed and affectionate political biography, as is *Harold Macmillan* (Weidenfeld and Nicolson, 1982) by Sir Nigel Fisher, a Conservative member and friend of Mr Macmillan.

*Wyndham and Children First*, by the late Lord Egremont (John Wyndham), was published by Macmillan in 1968 and includes many happy and amusing memories of working for Mr Macmillan. *Downing Street Diary* (Hodder and Stoughton, 1981) is a fascinating and detailed account of the late Sir Harold Evans's term as Mr Macmillan's Adviser on Public Relations during his Prime Ministership.

Alistair Horne, the distinguished historian, has been at work for some years on the official biography, which will be published after Mr Macmillan's death. Horne has enjoyed full access to the private archives and also, a unique blessing for a biographer, to the subject himself.

# *Index*

Numbers in *italics* refer to illustrations. Pictures in which Harold Macmillan or Lady Dorothy appear are not individually indexed.

**Picture Acknowledgements**
Associated Newspapers: 13 below, 120. Associated Press: 88, 135, 137 above, 159. Balliol College Archives: 12. BBC Copyright: 128. BBC Hulton Picture Library: 22, 32, 33, 44, 45 top, 75, 94–5. Ralph Crane, *Life* Magazine © Time Inc., 1960: 142. Crown Copyright/COI: 72, 100, 101 below, 146, 147. *Daily Express*: 99, 166, 174. *Daily Mail*: 131 centre, 171. *Evening Standard*: 80. John Frost Collection: 40. John Hillelson Agency/photo Raymond Darolle: 109. Imperial War Museum: 52, 58, 59, 60, 62, 63, 64, 65 above, 66. John Keeling: 160 below. Keystone Press: 47, 82, 94, 98, 105, 111, 123, 129 below, 131 below, 158 right, 160 above, 164, 167. P.S.H. Lawrence Eton Collection: 9. *Lincolnshire Echo*: 55. *London Evening News*: 131 above. Joseph McKeown/Colorific: 106–7. The Macmillan Family Archives: i, ii, xii, 2, 3, 4, 5, 6, 7, 8, 10, 13 above, 14–15, 16, 19, 25, 26, 27, 29, 34, 35, 36, 37, 38, 39, 45 below, 48, 50, 51, 54, 65 bottom, 67, 69, 74, 78, 79, 101 above, 103, 104, 112, 113, 114–15, 116, 117, 118, 119, 121, 126, 129 above, 130, 132, 134, 136, 137 below, 138–9, 140, 144, 145, 150, 156, 161 above, 162, 170. North of England Newspapers: 43, 70. Popperfoto: 157. Press Association: 41, 108, 122,125, 152, 172, 176, 178. Private Collections: 158 left, 169. Snowdon: 168. Sport and General: 84–5, 86, 92, 124, 153, 161 below. *Sun* Newspaper: 148. *Sunday Times*: 97. Times Newspapers: 42. Feliks Topolski: 83. Douglas Weaver: 155.

Between pages 6–7, 30–31: The Macmillan Family Archives. Between pages 126–7: Karsh of Ottawa/Camera Press. John Hillelson Agency/photo Michael Hardy. John Hillelson Agency/(above) photo Michael Hardy and (below right) photo George Rodger/ Magnum. Private Collection, below left. The Macmillan Family Archives, above. Keystone Press, below. Between pages 174–5: University of Oxford, above. Thomas Photos, Oxford, below. Keystone Press. Camera Press/photo Terence Spencer.

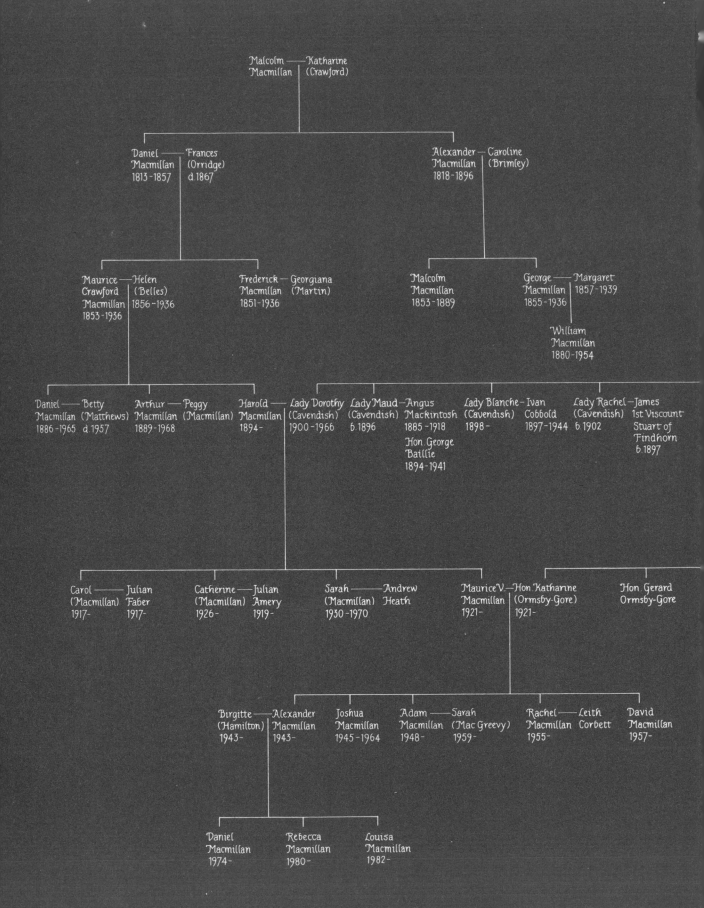